Get
Off
Your
Assets!

Get Off Your Assets!

How to Deal
with the
Challenges
of Life—and
Win!

Desi
Williamson

Andrews McMeel
Publishing

Kansas City

01 02 03 04 05 QUF 10 9 8 7 6 5 4 3 2 1

Library of Congress Cataloging-in-Publication Data
Williamson, Desi.
Get off your assets! : how to deal with the challenges of life and win / Desi Williamson.
    p. cm.
ISBN 0-7407-2013-9
1. Success—Psychological aspects. 2. Success in business. I. Title.

BF637.S8 W517 2001
158.1—dc21

2001046056

CONTENTS

ACKNOWLEDGMENTS

Writing a book stretches you so much, because it forces you to dig deep to find ways to express yourself when you're exhausted and out of emotional fuel; it is clearly one of the toughest things that I've ever had to do. Here's to all of the people who filled my tank when it was empty. I want to thank my mother, Ann, who gave me life; it's great to have you in my life again. I want to say thanks and I love you to my family, the members of which put up with so many inconveniences in helping me realize my dreams. To my wife, Sue, who provided much-needed inspiration. To my daughter, Talia, and son, Reece, who are my heart and soul and give me the strength to reach greater heights because I want them to as well.

To my grandmother Nonnie, because she believed in me when nobody else did, gave me a home, loved me unconditionally, and gave me a chance to make something of my life. To my father, Maurice, who instilled in me a real work ethic and who taught me that anything in life worth having is worth working for. To all of my uncles, who taught me what being a "real man" is all about.

I want to thank Renée Strom for discovering me and seeing things in me I didn't see in myself. She accelerated my career through her guidance and support. And lastly, I want to thank all of the mentors throughout my career who, through their own examples, have helped to set the standards by which I measure myself. To outstanding people such as Jim Rohn, Zig Ziglar, Tony Robbins, John Johnson, Tom Hopkins, Keith Harrell, John Alston, Danielle Kennedy, Jack Canfield, Mark Victor Hansen, Og Mandino, Robert Schuller, the National Speakers Association, Les Brown, Rick Rainbolt, Michael Chatman, Randy Gage, Dr. Jeffrey Lant, Harvey Mackay, and so many others who have made a difference in my life. I also want to thank my good friend Victory Smith, as well as Saunni Dais Productions, for thought-provoking poetry that helped me through tough days completing this project. Let us continue to be messengers of hope in making the world a better place.

INTRODUCTION:
IT'S WHERE YOU'RE GOING THAT COUNTS!

> When you are inspired by some great purpose, some extraordinary project, all your thoughts break their bounds: Your mind transcends limitations, your consciousness expands in every direction, and you find yourself in a new, great, and wonderful world. Dormant forces, faculties, and talents become alive, and you discover yourself to be a greater person by far than you ever dreamed yourself to be.
>
> —Patanjali

The purpose of this book is to help you unleash the power within you to achieve your dreams. Everyone should have a dream. We all grow up with dreams of what we want to be; but by adulthood, the harsh realities of life have set in, and many of us have become cynical about the present and apprehensive about the future. Some have given up on life because of past failures, bad influences, negative people in their lives, factors related to their race, or a host of other influences. They don't believe they have a future.

The threat of unemployment, fueled by changes in corporate business structures, has many people scared about the future. At the same time, opportunity abounds! There are more ways to succeed in today's world because there has never been more information and technology available to those with the ambition to seek out success, the discipline to learn, the courage to take action, and the persistence to continue until they reach their destination.

Many fail because they are frozen in fear. They don't take action. They find themselves sitting on the sidelines of life. Fear causes them to settle for less than they could be or less than they could have. They don't believe in possibilities. They don't seek out the people or information that could help them reach their goals. Could this be you?

Get Off Your Assets! How to Deal with the Challenges of Life—and Win! is a book about self-empowerment and personal development.

I want you to know that regardless of your situation, you have the power to succeed. It's a matter of what you focus on, how determined you are to have it, and the strategies you employ to get it.

Every person has a wealth of potential, and we all have unique gifts. Many people I come across during my travels readily admit they are using only a fraction of their potential. This is probably true, to some extent, for all of us.

I want to help you get your dreams back—the dreams you've had but dared not entertain, out of fear that success was something that happened only to other people. As we go forward, let's keep in mind that the concept of motivation, and motivational speaking in particular, have come under fire recently. People get excited after reading a motivational book or leaving an uplifting seminar, but they wonder, "Where do I go from here? What do I do next?" If you're not careful, it won't be long before the good feelings you get from my message will be gone, and you'll again find yourself struggling for emotional survival.

A Life's Lesson

In the 1950s and 1960s, my environment was totally black. Unless I ventured downtown, I could go for weeks and never see a person of a different race. Black people owned the local businesses—including the department stores, barbershops, grocery stores, restaurants, gas stations, taverns, and shoe-shine parlors. I can still remember going to my cousin Vernon's barbershop on Sunday afternoon and learning from the older men as they discussed everything from sports to politics.

Even with this positive influence, it was apparent to me that the household I lived in was different. Most of the children in my St. Louis neighborhood came from typical families, with a mother, father, and two or three children—or sometimes as many as ten. My mother was only sixteen years old when I was born, and my father was nineteen. You might say that we grew up together—babies raising a baby. I can vaguely remember my mother and father living together for a short period of time. We had a three-bedroom house with a living room, kitchen, and bedroom all lined up like dominoes. An old kerosene-burning stove was supposed to heat the whole house, but it rarely did, and I burned myself on it frequently, even though I was instructed not to play near it. My crib was in the same room as my mother and father's bed. I can still see the shadows cast on the walls and ceiling while that old stove hummed, growing hotter and hotter.

My mother had two other children, my brother André and my sister, Kumonte. André was always tough, and even as a kid, man, he loved to fight. My mother had a rule: When she was at work, we were, under no condition, to be at someone else's house. One day when we were over at a friend's house down the street, my mother came home earlier than we expected. She called outside for us, as she always did. We started to run out of our friend's house, but André didn't notice there was a glass storm door in front of him. He smashed right through it. He emerged with a huge piece of glass jutting out of his stomach that would have caused most adults to pass out. He pulled the glass out of his stomach and didn't wince or cry. He was only four years old.

This would have a profound effect on me. I had known for a long time that there were problems. By my third birthday, my mother and father had divorced. She was caught between trying to be a mother and living the life of the young woman. Always attracted to men who were abusive, alcoholic, and drug users, with few exceptions, she went on to marry a total of nine times—and always had boyfriends in between. She was desperately searching for something and running from herself. I would later run from myself as well.

Many times, she would stay out all night on weekends, leaving me at home alone. She would tell me to lock the door and not answer it even if Jesus Christ himself knocked on it. I was so lonely and scared I would find myself running up and down the street screaming and crying until the neighbors brought me in. They would keep me until she came back, and the cycle would start all over again.

My mother married a semipro basketball player after my parents separated. When he drank, which was frequently, he beat my mother badly. I remember being locked out of the house in the cold one winter day. I stood outside, knocking on the door for what seemed like forever, freezing. I knew he was in the house and wondered why he didn't answer. When he finally swung open the door, he snatched me inside and slapped me until my nose started to bleed—for waking him up because I wanted to come in out of the cold.

After many of these beatings, he threatened me further by telling me that if I said anything to my mother, he would beat me even worse. This pattern repeated itself through several of my mother's marriages, and it forced me to grow up quicker than I should have had to. I learned how to cook, clean a house, wash clothes and diapers, and take care of my little brother and sister. While most kids came home from school to play with their friends, I cooked dinner, cleaned house, and readied my brother and sister for the next day. I was eight years old!

Finally, my mother married a man I just couldn't stand. He beat and kicked my mother in front of me. They would make up, but he always did the same thing again. They had wild parties rife with drugs and booze, and the house wound up a mess every time. I was always cleaning up the aftermath, and then going to the Laundromat to wash clothes for everyone—my mother, this guy, my little brother and sister, and myself. I thought about killing him while he was asleep, but I could never muster the courage. I made up my mind that I couldn't deal with it anymore and wanted out.

Since I was a small child, I had frequently gone over to my grandmother's house to visit. Whenever it was time to leave, I cried because I didn't want to go back home to the negative atmosphere around my mother and her men. But I felt sorry for my mother. She was searching for love, and her children paid the price along with her for her choices.

Then, on April 17, 1968, I did something that transformed my life. My mother told me to clean up the house after another party while the abuser was in the bedroom asleep. I cleaned that house until it shined like new money. I knew it would be the last time. I was getting out of there! I was leaving for my own survival, physical and emotional. I had been a sad little boy for a long time. I wanted a chance at happiness. I knew there had to be something better.

When I finished cleaning, I packed my clothes in brown paper grocery bags, called a cab, and left for my grandmother's house. One of the hardest decisions I've ever had to make was to leave my little brother and sister as I rode off in that cab, but at the age of eleven, I couldn't take them with me. My father had legal custody of me, but no rights to my brother or sister. My grandmother told me she would have taken them along with me, but that the authorities could take them back. It was at this point that I was truly born and from which I have become the person I am today. I'm certain that had my grandmother not taken me, I would be on drugs, in jail, or dead.

Successful people are often perceived to be perfect, with perfect, happy lives. Nothing could be further from the truth! Many often have stories like mine, filled with sadness and misfortune.

This pain compels us to make a difference in the world by helping others to see that, regardless of their past circumstances, they can realize their dreams. You can use your past either as a crutch or as a launchpad to a brighter future. Let the pain in your life make you smarter, stronger, wiser, and more caring. I am grateful for everything that has happened to me. In those misfortunes, I was able to explore depths of my being that might have gone undiscovered.

In moments of challenge, you will find the courage that lets you know that, with God's help, you can handle anything. When you come to accept your past as a learning- and character-building experience, you move from the realm of blame and condemnation to one of living life to the fullest, with the goal of becoming all you can be. It is through the sharing of pain, which is part of the human experience, that you learn to appreciate the sweetness of victory. The more obstacles you encounter and overcome, the more character you will develop as a result. The more character you develop, the bigger the contribution you can make toward leaving this world a better place than you found it.

Success is not in short supply. It's available in abundance, and it is your God-given right! I want to give you some how-tos, coupled with your own individual action plan, on this journey to empowering yourself to achieve your dreams. Read this book with an open mind. Take from it the ideas you like, consider the rest, and then take *massive* action toward building your life to order.

I'm confident this book will help you find hope, empowerment, and possibilities for your life. I want you to realize you are a special person with your own unique gifts. The world needs them! Perhaps in these pages you will find the courage to discover and share your gifts and life's most powerful elixir—hope.

CHAPTER 1
THE POWER OF PURPOSE

*Trial Boss, from whom
do you receive your
government?*

*The Will in overdrive,
focused with carnivorous
intent!*

*What is the purpose
of the path you have cleared
and blazed?*

*My Will hath one burden . . .
to mirror that upon which
it has glazed!*

—**Saunni Dais**

> *Far better is it to dare to do great things, to win glorious triumphs even though checkered by failure, rather than join the ranks of those poor miserable souls who neither suffer much nor enjoy much, for they live in the gray dim twilight that knows neither victory nor defeat.*
>
> **—Charles Bernard Shaw**

When I was younger, I was a terrible athlete. I wanted so much to be a football star, but I was small, slow, and not very aggressive. I wanted a way out of the negative environment surrounding me: poverty, drugs, and violence. So I set my sights on a goal, a vision, a journey into a better life. I knew that a football scholarship would give me that chance.

It's strange sometimes how an unfortunate incident can lead to something very good. I was put back from the fifth to the fourth grade because in Missouri the law dictated that when a child moved from the city to the suburbs, the child was automatically put back one grade. I think this sprang from a belief that suburban schools were so superior to city schools the transferred student would not be able to keep up.

I was destroyed. I felt stupid, as if I had really done something wrong. I couldn't do anything right. All the other kids seemed to be smarter, better looking, and to have more athletic skills than me. I went out for Little League football and got pounded into the ground.

The other kids laughed at me because I was so awkward. I will never forget trying to tackle a kid named Jimmy Williams. He was like a little ten-year-old version of Jim Brown. When I tried to tackle him one day in practice, he ran over me as if I were a gnat and bloodied my nose.

I cried during the bus ride home that night because everyone at practice had made fun of me, told me I was a scrub and had no chance to make the team. I was a laughingstock. I've never been so humiliated. The next day I quit to avoid the embarrassment of being cut. It ate at my soul for an entire year. I was a quitter! I swore that the next year I would go out for football again and not quit again, no matter what.

All that winter I dreamed of making the team. It became an obsession. I saw myself succeeding, and through trial and error discovered something that would serve me for the rest of my life: the power of visualization. When the next year came, I made the team and was one of its best players, but not one of the best athletes. I would come to practice early and stay late. I worked on my own outside of practice. I slept, ate, and drank football.

I found that if I was dedicated enough to something, I would eventually find a way to succeed. Seven years later, as a senior in high school, I showed up on the *St. Louis Post-Dispatch*'s All-Metro Team and on other all-star teams. I can't remember how many people said, "Is that Desi Williamson? I don't believe it. He was a horrible athlete as a kid."

I'll never forget running into Jimmy Williams, the superstar Little League player, shortly after appearing in the Sunday edition of the newspaper. I hadn't seen him since Little League. I stood a full head taller and outweighed him by at least forty pounds. I was the star, and he was the one who stared in envy. He couldn't believe how I had changed! I left feeling so good and learned a valuable lesson: *Just because things are doesn't necessarily mean they will always be.*

We all develop at different times in our lives and should never judge ourselves based on our current circumstances, because that does not represent the sum total of what we can become. In that thought we should find all of the encouragement we need to keep on truckin'.

You Don't Always Get What You Want

I was fortunate enough to be awarded several scholarships to different schools around the country and chose the University of Minnesota. Although the football program was not the greatest, they did compete in the Big Ten, and I saw the chance to play and earn a letter as a freshman (which I ultimately did). I reasoned that I could go to one of various other schools and possibly play in a bowl game every year, but where would I live when football was over? Most of the other big schools were located in small towns where the opportunities would be limited when the band stopped playing. When I looked at the whole package, few schools in the country matched the University of Minnesota.

Every blue-chip athlete in the country has the dream of playing in the National Football League, and I was certainly no different. I became a starting linebacker seven games into my freshman season in the Big

Ten, playing against schools like Michigan, Ohio State, and Nebraska. A year before, I had been watching these guys on TV, and now here I was, one of them. I just knew that four years later, I would be right there on Sundays, with all of my friends and family watching me run up and down the fields of the NFL.

One of the most disappointing days of my life came during the 1978 NFL draft. I sat there by the phone waiting for it to ring, but it never did. By the time the end of the last round of the draft rolled around, it became apparent that my lifelong dream was not going to happen. I was devastated. Everything I thought about myself was wrapped up in football: my self-esteem and my self-image.

It was the worst day of my life. The next day my body said, "Get up," and my mind asked, "For what?" I was so embarrassed because playing in the NFL was something I thought others expected of me. I felt as though I had let them down. To make matters worse, two of my "best friends" came over to my house to roast me. They said, "Let's cheer for the next star linebacker in the NFL. Ha! Ha! Ha!" I wanted someplace to hide.

They were actually doing me a big favor. Both of these guys had been through the same thing the year before. They had been high school all-Americans and stars at the University of Minnesota but also had not made it to the ranks of the NFL. As painful as it was, they were helping me. I had to learn to move on. One of my friends told me that if going to the NFL would be the highlight of my life, I was in for a sorry life. How right he was!

Critical Decisions

At the University of Minnesota, I was a utility man. I played linebacker my first two years, defensive end my junior year, and started at right offensive guard my senior year. Offensive linemen in major college football at the time weighed between 250 and 275 pounds; I played the position at a stout 205 pounds. I'd always believed in the concept of "team" and played wherever the coach felt was best for the program.

The last move cost me dearly in the draft. The NFL drafts players by position, and no team in the land was going to draft a lineman the size of a running back. I had an agent, however, who tried to position me as a player who could do it all, a sort of jack-of-all-trades. He was able to get two offers, one from the St. Louis Cardinals (now the Arizona Cardinals) in my hometown and one from the Cincinnati Bengals. Both teams said they would pay me the standard scale for training camp and offered me a contract of $28,000 if I made the team.

I told my agent to forget it. I knew I could get a sales job that would pay me the same, only I wouldn't have to risk my life in the process. It was one of the best decisions I've ever made. I had to develop other interests. Getting my degree became more important than ever. I had always been a good student, and I went back to class even more committed. I was not going to let myself off the hook by not graduating. That would have been much more embarrassing than not making the pros.

This allowed me to put football in proper perspective. Many of my teammates went on to get drafted. I was envious, but I knew one thing: Every athlete's career has a limited life expectancy. Some aren't forced to deal with the reality of life until they are in their middle or late thirties. For some, it's hard to adjust when the cheering stops and they are no longer the center of attention. Some jocks never get over it.

I felt that the sooner I wrestled with those demons and settled the score, the better off I'd be. A few years later, some of the guys who had gone on to the pros were retired, with blown-out knees, constant migraine headaches, and worn-out spirits. I still had my health and a new lease on life. I realize now that not getting drafted was one of the best things that ever happened to me.

When things don't go as we think they should, we need to remember that life is a book with many chapters. As one closes, another opens, giving us the opportunity to discover parts of ourselves we would not have known had we struggled to hold on to things after it was time to give them up. This is true with a job, a relationship, or any major decision in life. When we open our eyes, we find that one situation will often lead to another more exciting one, if we are willing to let go.

Winners Practice the Art of Adjusting

Have you ever really been looking forward to something that didn't happen? Perhaps a big sale fell through, a date was canceled, or a promotion didn't materialize? What did you do? Did you lie down and die, or did you get off your assets and crank the effort up even higher?

I was on a flight one evening from Miami to Minneapolis when the plane hit some turbulence. It was enough to make me grab that little bag and lose my cookies. After we were on the ground, it occurred to me that the pilot had not turned the plane around and gone back home. He'd made a slight adjustment to get us out of that turbulent air and safely to our destination.

Sometimes in business or in our personal lives, things don't happen the way we think they should. Sometimes our best-laid plans don't work out; and when they don't, you need to be prepared to make adjustments to correct your course. Sometimes you have to take a detour or a path that was not in your original plan.

Hollywood, Here I Come!

I've always been a believer in the saying "Shoot for the moon and land on a star." After not making it in the NFL, I packed up my bags and moved to Hollywood. I had visited Los Angeles previously, and I was excited by the hoopla surrounding Hollywood. It's exhilarating for anyone the first time.

Driving east to west down Wilshire Boulevard, you'll find drastic differences in economic conditions as you travel through the Crenshaw district to Beverly Hills and finally to the ocean. At a street called San Vicente, you notice an immediate transformation. You are now on the outskirts of Beverly Hills. The moment you cross this street, everything changes. Every car is a Mercedes, BMW, Ferrari, Maserati, Rolls-Royce, or Lexus. In fact, the Mercedes is known as the Volkswagen of Beverly Hills. It's hard to believe that some can have so much and others so little and only be separated by a few city blocks.

My cousin Fred Williamson, better known as "the Hammer," had fashioned himself a good career in the movies after playing for several years with the Kansas City Chiefs. I figured I was better looking than he and that all I needed was a shot.

I had a couple of things going for me, too. I had earned my Screen Actors Guild and American Federation of Television and Radio Artists union cards in Minneapolis. In Hollywood, to get that speaking part in a movie, you've got to be in the union; and in order to get in the union, you've got to have had a speaking part on TV or in a movie. I had both. I went on audition after audition, and was fortunate enough to sign on with an improv comedy group called the L.A. Connection. I also did some commercial work, hawking different products for various companies, in print ads mostly, and on TV.

There's a very dark side to Hollywood. I went on several auditions that turned out to be cattle calls for pornographic movies. I was shocked to learn how many young men and women went to L.A. with the goal of stardom and ended up making a deal with the devil. Plus, there were tons of acting and voice coaches of all types that offered to help you make your dreams come true—for a small fee of course. After the Tinseltown tinsel tarnished, I understood that Hollywood preys upon the element in people that craves love and attention; there's almost a sickness to wanting to be a film or television star so badly that you would literally do anything to get there. And many people do.

I saw many people that you would recognize from various movies at parties, in bars, and in restaurants. I learned that many people equate seeing someone on television or in a movie with that person having "made it." The fact is that one television or movie role does not make a career. This hit me squarely in the face at a restaurant one night in West Hollywood. I went to the bathroom and noticed a gentleman standing in the next stall who was a featured actor in the movie *Lady Sings the Blues*, starring Diana Ross. He looked like a bum off the streets and didn't display the signs of success associated with major-motion-picture employment. I asked if he was who I thought he was, and he said yes. I asked how he was doing, and he immediately began to give me a seminar on Hollywood. He told me that most of the "actors" in Hollywood were starving while they waited for their big break. Even among the ones that worked frequently, unless they were able to score a successful television series or work regularly in movies, they just barely scratched out a living. With the cost of living in Los Angeles, he said, unless you were willing to make a sacrifice and possibly risk the better part of your youth to pursue a career in the business, you should really rethink your plans. He warned that a struggling actor might end up waiting too long for something that might not be forthcoming or even worth it in the end. He mentioned he had several friends who'd wasted the best years of their lives trying to break into movies and who'd had their hearts and spirits broken.

At the age of twenty-four, I decided that I was not willing to sacrifice my youth for something I had little or no control over. I wanted to establish a life for myself that would give me a foundation for the future.

The Law of Distinctions

I don't want to discourage anyone who wishes to make acting a career. I found I had to discover my true motivation for wanting something; I had to find the right reasons. Only then could I determine what price I was really willing to pay in order to get what I wanted.

This distinction is the difference between success and failure in any calling. You must decide whether you want something because it's a labor of love or because you want the end result. If you only want the end result, you won't be able to deal with the obstacles you'll encounter in your journey. I went to Hollywood because I thought acting and being on television was cool. I didn't realize that most people who made it were willing to roll the dice with their futures to make it happen. I'd have had to be willing to sacrifice for as long as it took to succeed. I didn't love acting enough to put myself through the paces; I was impatient and not willing to live like a pauper. I had a great time out there but decided to move on. Had I not gone, I would have lived with regret for the rest of my life.

The ability to make distinctions allows you to move on to a more desirable station without wasting valuable time on something that is not in alignment with what you're committed to or willing to sacrifice for. Whatever it is you want to do with your life, I encourage you to just *go for it!* That's how you are going to be able to make judgments about what is right or wrong for you. We never really fail at anything; we make distinctions on what course is the right one for us. Life is like a smorgasbord, and the only way you can find out what different foods taste like is to put them in your mouth and chew.

Got an Itch? Quit Complainin' and Start Scratchin'!

We all reach forks in the road where critical decisions determine the course of our lives. I decided that the best course for me was to build a career in sales. Sales was exciting. It involved dealing with people, and I love people. It also took advantage of some of the skills most agreeable to my personality, and it involved some degree of acting, because in order to deliver a presentation, I had to put a certain amount of showmanship to work. It was clearly one of the best decisions I've ever made. I've worked for three of the top Fortune 500 companies in the country and achieved success in my own businesses. This also led me to my true calling in life—the professional-speaking and management-training business.

I've had great jobs with great companies: Johnson & Johnson, Johnson Wax Company, Rain Bird Sprinkler, Pepsi-Cola, and Cadbury Schweppes. I also worked many other jobs, but always felt compelled to leave once I felt I had plateaued. I had a chronic itch that needed to be scratched, and the remedy was always an opportunity to learn something new.

People are often afraid to make changes in their lives because they are comfortable with what they have. Unfortunately, if you don't have a dream that's bigger than your current situation, you will never grow and realize what your true potential is. Some people might have thought that my moving around so much was career suicide. That might have been true if not for changes in the last thirty years. It used to be that having more than three jobs in five years was the kiss of death. Now if you don't have a varied background with different levels of experience, you've got a problem. Everything changes!

You've got to have a game plan and know in advance what your outcome is going to be. You've got to have the courage to make a move when you get that itch that's sure to come. If you can anticipate your itches in advance, you can be prepared to change the course of your life when you sense that things are no longer meeting your expectations.

Sand in the Hourglass

With every job I ever had, I envisioned an hourglass. When that last grain of sand flowed out of the top of the hourglass, I knew it was time for me to move on. I think subconsciously I did this because I wanted to maintain control over my life and what happened to me. I had a gnawing feeling that there was something more out there for me, and not moving at the right time meant I was losing ground. The hourglass concept will allow you to take control of your life by anticipating what your next move is going to be rather than waiting to see what will happen. Chances are it won't be much.

Layoffs will continue to be a part of the American employment landscape, and companies everywhere are telling people to become empowered to take control of their future. Lifetime employment is a thing of the past.

Corporations are not out to deliberately ruin your life; they must continue to reinvent themselves to remain competitive and stay in business in this global economy. You must be willing to corral your future and make the appropriate move at the right time. Make sure that you always give more than you take in everything that you do. Give your employer everything you have to offer. Learn as much as you can, and use what you've learned to craft a better future for yourself and your family. You must operate with enlightened self-interest. It's just a reality of life. You will be that much further ahead in the game.

You Need a Personal Challenge

For the longer I live, the more convinced I become that the biggest difference between the feeble and the powerful, the great and insignificant, is will, a purpose once fixed, and then victory or death.

—Anonymous

Have you ever read a motivational book, gone to a seminar, or listened to some tapes and felt energized? More than likely you felt as if you could tackle the world, didn't you? What happened after a short period of time? If you're like most people, you found that the feeling didn't last. As soon as you hit your first adversity, your attitude was right back where it had started. That's because being truly motivated comes from more than just a feeling.

In order for electricity to work properly, a circuit must be grounded with a grounding wire. Only then will it transfer the proper amount of current to the right locations. Motivation is the same way. It must be grounded in a thing called *purpose*—a goal strived for with determination. Without one, you will find yourself a frustrated person who drifts aimlessly through life taking whatever comes your way, usually after the people who have a definite purpose have dined at the table of opportunity.

Many times, purpose can be manifested by circumstances. The first key is to ask six basic questions. You must determine:

1. Who can help you in your mission?

2. What do you want and what do you need to do to get it?

3. When will you take the necessary action?

4. Where will the action take place?

5. Why are you involved in this activity? Why do you want this?

6. How will you go about taking the action that will address or solve the problem?

I believe that each of us must be compelled by some kind of personal challenge. Even if you aren't crystal clear on the challenge, these questions will cause you to think. If you keep asking these questions about whatever you deal with, you'll find the personal challenge that will ultimately lead to your purpose in life.

If there's a mountain, someone will try to climb it. If there's a river, no matter how wide, somebody will try to cross it. And if there's a record, somebody will eventually break it. Take the four-minute mile. Since the beginning of track and field, it was thought humanly impossible to run the mile in under four minutes. Then on May 6, 1954, Roger Bannister broke the barrier by running the mile in 3:59.4. Interestingly, since Bannister did it, many others have also run the mile in under four minutes. After Bannister achieved this milestone, other people had a stronger conviction than ever before. They created in themselves a stronger purpose because someone else had demonstrated what could be done.

Another example is the football rushing record of Jim Brown of the Cleveland Browns. He rushed for more than 12,000 yards in his nine-year career. His record stood for almost twenty years, until Walter Payton of the Chicago Bears came along and blew that record away with more than 16,000 yards. Why had so many others failed to break the barrier before Payton? Brown played with more conviction and purpose than anyone else before him. He played the game with a sense of purpose and commitment rarely seen since.

Brown once said in an interview that many players in today's game don't have passion. They run out of bounds, lie on the field, and accept being hurt. Other players are so concerned about getting hurt that they don't go all out each and every time their cleats touch the field. If you ever saw Brown run, you know what I'm talking about. It was a thing of beauty. He ran over, under, very seldom around, and most of the time straight through the opposing players to get to that end zone. I don't recall him ever running out of bounds to avoid contact. Payton played with the same level of intensity and purpose.

Greatness in any form requires performing with a greater sense of purpose than anyone else. It takes that level of commitment to succeed. There were many players who were faster, stronger, and had better talent surrounding them than Jim Brown and Walter Payton. Purpose is an intangible that can't be measured, but one thing is certain: When a person has it, extraordinary things happen!

I do not wish to walk smooth paths or travel an easy road.
I pray for strength and fortitude (that) I may bear the heavy load.
I pray for strength (that) I may climb the highest peaks alone
and transfer every stumbling block into a stepping stone.

—Anonymous

Jackie Robinson and His Purpose

Another example of purpose is the Jackie Robinson story. It was August 25, 1946, and Branch Rickey, the general manager of the Brooklyn Dodgers, was staring out of the window with a vision. He was sickened by the amount of prejudice, hate, and malice in the world, particularly as it related to major league baseball. At that time, blacks were not allowed to play in the major leagues and were relegated to playing in the Negro League. This infuriated Rickey, who believed that baseball was an American sport, and that every citizen, regardless of race or cultural background, should have the opportunity to compete in that great game. Rickey also had a hidden agenda. He knew that this would help break a pattern of bigotry in society as a whole, and that baseball would be the perfect metaphor.

As Rickey thought about who would be the first black man to break into the majors, one name kept coming into his mind with almost monotonous regularity. The name was Jackie Robinson. Late that afternoon, Robinson and Rickey sat across the desk from each other, eyeball to eyeball. Finally, Rickey asked Robinson if he could do it, if he could play with the Dodgers the next season. Robinson was puzzled. Rickey explained that what they would try to do together would meet with resistance: People would try to destroy the goodwill intended by the act; Robinson's teammates would attempt to sabotage him; fans would spit in his face. "They will call you a nigger! And what's more, Jackie, you can't fight back!" Rickey explained to Robinson that if he were to fight back, it would solidify the stereotype that black people could not perform under pressure. Rickey explained that the focus would be taken off Robinson's playing and placed on his behavior, and he informed Robinson that his play on the field would have to do all of the talking.

Robinson proved more than up to the challenge. As Rickey had promised, Robinson's detractors came in all forms. Opposing players spit chewing tobacco at his face when passing him on the field. Pitchers threw fastballs at his head when he was in the batter's box. He was not allowed to eat in the same restaurants with the team, and he frequently had to stay with friends or family because the team's hotels would not let him register. Many times, other baseball teams threatened to boycott the game if the Dodgers showed up with Robinson in the lineup. On one occasion, his own team members threatened to boycott play unless Robinson was released. They too had miscalculated the power of purpose and of an idea whose time had come. Rickey went on to conduct a team meeting in which he verbally ripped them apart. He asked the perpetrators where their parents came from; many said their parents were immigrants who came to America in search of a better life. Rickey then asked those players what right their parents had to pursue the American dream if they believed that people should be refused the opportunity to play a great American sport such as baseball because of the color of their skin. Rickey went on to further inform them that Robinson would play on the team, with or without them.

As Rickey had promised, the public did their part by ripping Robinson in the press and to his face, and by doing anything they could think up to get him to retaliate, but he always heard a voice reverberating in his head. It was the voice of Branch Rickey, reminding him, "Remember, Jackie, no matter what, you can't fight back! You've gotta let your play on the field do the talking!" Robinson went on to become major league baseball's rookie of the year that year and its most valuable player two years later. Every time you see a Barry Bonds, Dave Justice, Benito Santiago, or Kirby Puckett step to the plate and take a swipe at that ball, remember that it all got started because two men of different races who were filled with purpose met in a room in 1946 and made a decision that changed the world.

If they could do all of that in spite of the ignorance they faced at that time, do you think it's possible for you to make a difference in this world? The answer is: *Absolutely!*

You've Got to Keep On Keepin' On

Whenever I feel sorry for myself, I think about certain people who really paid the price, some with their lives, so that you and I might have an easier go of it: Abraham Lincoln, John F. Kennedy, Martin Luther King Jr., Mahatma Gandhi, and Mother Teresa. These leaders felt so strongly about their purposes in life that they were willing to die for them. Once you identify your purpose, you'll find it hard not to be excited, to get up early, and stay up late. You will find a fire burning deep within you.

I think about my grandmother Nonnie, the lady who raised me. She had eight children by the time she was twenty-four years old. My grandfather kicked her out of their house in the back hills of Tennessee, took all the children, and left her with no money and no place to go. She borrowed enough money from her family to catch a bus to St. Louis, where she found a job as a cook and housekeeper for a wealthy family earning thirty-two dollars a week.

When she told me this story, Nonnie explained that getting her children back was her reason for living. It became an all-consuming purpose backed by a burning desire. She created what amounted to an Underground Railroad as she sought to free her children from the wrath of my grandfather. Nonnie would save her money and go pick up one or two of them; then she'd retreat, save a little more money, and go back to get the others, by plane, train, or automobile.

What's significant about this is it took her seven years to get them all back, including my father. No matter how long it took, she was prepared to see her mission through. She had rough times; sometimes her integrity was tested, as when men from the wealthy family she worked for propositioned her. She risked her job to maintain her standards. In the end, she got her children back, and she later used this same energy to give me a chance in life to make something of myself.

You may have family stories like these, about heroes or heroines who succeeded despite what seemed to be insurmountable odds. Chances are, the greater the odds were, the stronger that person's purpose and burning desire were. Even when things seem hopeless, you've got to keep on keepin' on, knowing that whenever you have a purpose, your conviction will be tested.

People see me now, traveling across the country in first class, speaking to Fortune 500 companies, and assume I've led a charmed life. But what they see is what they think is a finished product. They don't see the pain and turmoil I've endured to become the person I am now. More importantly, they don't see what paces I'm willing to put myself through to continue to grow and develop into the person I wish to be.

If my grandmother could do all she did with limited resources, as did the people in your own families, and those throughout the course of history who overcame great obstacles so we could have a better life, don't you think it's possible for you to make a difference in the world with your own unique contribution? The answer is: *Absolutely!*

You have an obligation to do so. We are all in debt. The fact that you were born in or live in this country is a debt you can never repay. You owe it to your God to be successful, and you owe it to yourself to be successful, but most of all, you owe it to whoever may be watching you—because somebody always is.

A Man and His Dream

Reasons come first, answers come second.

—Jim Rohn

I often think about the incomparable inventor Preston Tucker. His example shows that you never know what having resounding purpose can lead to. Tucker invented the padded dashboard, disc brakes, seat belts, and fuel injection. The Tucker automobile was a 1940s phenomenon. It featured these enhancements, as well as headlights that would turn in tandem with the front wheels so you could see around dark corners at night. Aerodynamically, his design presaged the cars of today. The Tucker was way ahead of its time!

Tucker had invented a better mousetrap, and the Big Three automakers knew it. They were scared to death! Through the use of money, politics, and influence, the Big Three got together with the government. They tried to send Mr. Tucker to prison by claiming that he never intended to build a car but sold franchises to hopefuls with the idea of bilking them out of money.

Tucker was acquitted of all charges of fraud, but the court mandated that he could never build the car. Outside the courtroom sat fifty Tuckers in a rainbow of colors, the same ones that hours earlier he almost went to prison for never intending to build.

As the people attending the trial hopped into the cars for a ride, at an invitation extended by Tucker, Tucker's confidant said, "Look at the people, they love the cars! Preston, we could have built fifty million, but now there will only be fifty ever built." Tucker responded, "Fifty or fifty million, it's having a purpose; it's the dream that counts." Tucker went on to create automatic ice dispensers for refrigerators and many other inventions that helped improve the quality of life for many generations to come. His purpose was in clear view.

This brings me to what I call the Impact Law: From this day forward, promise you will ask of yourself continuously, "What is my purpose in life?" Sometimes negative things happen in your life. This will cause you to do one of two things: You can quit or you can continue to search for the answers necessary to discover your true purpose in life. From this process you will find those compelling reasons to take action toward becoming that extraordinary person who resides within you.

"You've Got to Have a Machanism!"

Sometimes when negative things happen, we feel as though we want to give up and go into a shell for the rest of our lives, vowing to never again attempt to succeed. You can certainly do that. Or you can set your jaw tighter and create new resolve to succeed with more energy and commitment than before.

I've learned that a clear purpose is often what separates winners from losers. I believe we should welcome adversity. It often stretches us, and we find a stronger purpose than we may have had before.

My father always used to say to me, "Son, if you want to succeed in life, you've got to have a machanism!" He meant "mechanism"—an instrument or process, physical or mental, by which something is done or comes into being—but he pronounced it "machanism." My father barely finished the eighth grade. While we didn't spend much time together as I was growing up, I'll never forget the example he set for me of his drive to succeed and accomplish his purpose. He had an incredible work ethic. He always held at least three jobs. He worked all day, slept three or four hours, and went on to the next job.

He did this for fifteen to twenty years, always dreaming of one day owning his own nightclub. Before I was born, he worked for the Oberman Shoe Company in St. Louis, which manufactured insoles for shoes and competed with Dr. Scholl's. The owner bought a machine that would better automate the production process, but nobody knew how to operate it. He was going on vacation, and before he left, my father asked to speak with him. My father made Mr. Oberman a proposition. He told Oberman he would figure out how to operate the machine and fill the warehouse with inventory by the time he returned from vacation—if Oberman would give him a small percentage of the profits for working overtime to make it happen. Laughing, old man Oberman agreed to the terms, figuring my father was just talking and would eventually give up in frustration.

When Oberman returned from vacation, he got the shock of his life. That warehouse was filled with insoles. His eyes grew to the size of silver dollars, and at that moment he understood that Maurice Williamson was no ordinary guy. When my father approached him about the deal they had made previously, Oberman reneged. He told my father he admired his ambition, but the one with the gold makes the rules. Oberman told my father he would never reach his maximum earning potential while working for someone else. Then he told my father he was welcome to stay or quit anytime.

It was then my father found resolution enough to pursue his purpose. Owning his own nightclub became a burning desire, an obsession! He got a job as a waiter, and in those days could earn $300 to $400 a night if he hustled. And he did! He worked almost around the clock, saving his money. Over the next ten years, he saved $120,000. He then bought three cabs, leasing two of them and driving one himself. He did that for three years, took the money from that venture, and bought a liquor store. When the city came and took the store property via eminent domain, he realized his dream.

He found a small building on Olive Street, on the main drag heading toward the Gateway Arch in downtown St. Louis. There were three buildings on either side of his small building, with two big parking lots adjacent. He opened his nightclub in 1968, when he was thirty-two. He eventually bought the other buildings, the parking lots, and finally the entire city block.

Maurice's Gold Coast Night Club has been in operation for more than thirty years. During that time, everyone from movie stars to government officials has crossed the threshold. He had found his *machanism*. Interestingly enough, he'd learned much about life from his days as a waiter. He had waited on multimillionaires and listened to their conversations. He'd learned what foods and wines they liked, and he'd become a gourmet cook in the process. But the entire time, he saw himself owning his own business. The steps in the interim were part of the process necessary to get the knowledge he needed.

Watching him, I saw what raw determination was all about. Since then, many St. Louis nightclubs have come and gone. Many times, a competitor has warned my father that his club will be the one to put my father out of business. Each time, he simply laughs with a shrug of the shoulders, as if to say, "I hope you have paid as many dues as I have to learn the game." His competitors usually close their clubs within a few months or years—because they only want the social status that comes with owning a nightclub and can't compete. Few understand the price that has to be paid to be a long-term player.

When he told me years ago that I had to have a "machanism," he meant that I had to find something I enjoyed doing and figure out a way to make my living doing it. Most people settle for the first job that comes along without really analyzing how the job can help them accomplish some larger purpose. They find themselves in a cycle of doing just enough to keep from getting fired, and the boss usually pays them just enough to keep them from quitting (if they're any good to begin with). After years of this, people usually find themselves frustrated and empty, because they had dreams that died on the vine. They live with the ghosts of opportunity lost.

You must find the discipline necessary to discover your purpose. This requires the courage to think big and to see yourself with a burning desire to achieve an objective born as purpose from those thoughts. From there, you will find the whys and subsequently the hows necessary to create your own "machanism."

Who Are You?

Here's an exercise: Find a nice quiet room where you won't be disturbed and get yourself a pen or pencil and a pad of notebook paper. Stay in the room until you find the answers to these two questions. Write the answers down as explicitly as you can.

Question Number One: Who am I? (What is my personal identity? What do I stand for?)

Rule: You cannot describe yourself by using labels, such as president of XYZ Corporation or doctor, lawyer, or Indian chief, because it's easy to hide behind them. Describe who you are without using labels; let the pen flow and write how you feel about yourself. If we were attending your funeral, what would you want said about you?

Key Learning: I usually find that people get very frustrated with this exercise because they are thinking, for the first time, about what should be a basic question. I ask people in my seminars to describe the emotions they felt going through this process. I request that they use only one word to communicate it, and to express that word as if they were introducing themselves to me using that emotion as their first name. In other words, I want them to say, "Hello, I'm frustrated," or "Hello, I'm scared"—or confused, courageous, energized, lonely, loved, forgotten, heartbroken, sad, mad, glad. . . .

It's amazing that people find themselves at a loss for words when they go through this exercise and their labels are taken away. Only then can they discover who they really are. Our identity is our grounding wire to living a balanced life and understanding the difference between the false and the real.

A person I really respect is Tony Dungy. He was one of the main reasons I attended the University of Minnesota. I was impressed with him because he truly has his head screwed on correctly.

Tony was a quarterback; we played together for three years in college, and we shared an apartment. Today he is a good friend. If you follow professional football, you know he was destined to become one of the NFL's superstar head coaches, and many consider him one of the brightest coaches in the game today. To those who know him, none of this comes as a surprise.

He played with the likes of Terry Bradshaw, Mean Joe Greene,

Franco Harris, and Lynn Swan. This was enough to impress anyone. But I found it hilarious that whenever we were out together and people asked Tony what he did, he'd respond in a deadpan manner, "I'm a laborer." He was deadly serious. He never bought into stardom, and he kept the reality of the game in the forefront of his mind. He used to tell me, "Professional football is a business, and you're only as good as your last hit record."

Tony thought the entire concept of stardom was ridiculous. He often commented, "A young man comes into the NFL looking for fame and fortune, but you better get the fortune, 'cause that fame ain't nothing!" I'll always love him for being real, and no matter how much notoriety he gets from being the best at what he does, to those of us who know him he'll always be simply "T.D." He's a perfect example of someone who, despite having to overcome obstacles, succeeded by being true to himself.

In this same room or quiet place, answer the next major question.

Question Number Two: What is your purpose in life?

Rule: Answer this question as if you could accomplish anything you desire. In doing this, approach this exercise as if failure does not exist. What would you write down as your purpose if you knew for certain you could have it? There's no such thing as failure! Don't spend any time worrying about the what-ifs; just write what comes to your mind. The first things you write are normally the truest representation of how you really feel.

After this, write a clarifying statement as it relates to these two questions:

1. Who are you? (This is your personal identity.)

2. What is your purpose? (What do you want to accomplish in your life?)

These two clarifying statements will help you chart a course toward building a future more in line with how you feel about life rather than taking whatever comes along.

My clarifying statements are as follows:

Who am I? (Desi's personal identity.) I am a kind, loving person who cares about others and wishes to communicate love through the art of persuasion and human interaction. I am an honest and trustworthy human being who believes in dreams, hard work, and success as a birthright. I am a focused, persistent individual who is not afraid of success or failure because I understand that one cannot exist without the other. I am a spiritual human being and believe in a power higher than myself. I believe my life is a direct reflection of how I think, dream, and behave. I have and will become what I think about most often.

What is my purpose? (What does Desi want to do with his life?) My purpose is to grow and to develop all of my skills to their full potential, and to learn and stretch myself to the maximum in order to achieve success and happiness in all areas of my life—mental, spiritual, health, family, and financial. I want to make a positive contribution to the world and leave each situation better than I found it.

Your purpose statement should focus on what it is you want to become. Once we are clear as to exactly what we want to do with ourselves, we then have a template on which to overlay our activity and accomplishments. More importantly, if the answers to these two questions really represent what you value most in terms of your identity and purpose, you will find the answers because you have first found the reasons.

> *To have a purpose is the true joy of life. To have a purpose that's recognized by yourself as a mighty one. To be a force of life, rather than a feverish little clod of ailments and grievances complaining that the world will not devote itself to making you happy.*
>
> **—Charles Bernard Shaw**

CHAPTER 2
PROGRAM YOURSELF FOR SUCCESS

Queens and Kings, let your wildest imaginings seduce for you brighter days. Relax your anger, close your eyes and smile, see all the happy children lost at play. Nurture your most positive ideals, your dreams and the wonderful things you envision. Those fueled by your heart's desires shall be done with focus and passion. Always be patient with yourself and others . . . this insight may help when you're feeling down. You are one of the gifted and spirited, focus on your vision and it shall abound.

—Saunni Dais

Your imagination is your preview of life's coming attractions.

—Albert Einstein

M any critics of the motivational-speaking industry claim that moti-vation is like taking a warm bath: As soon as the bath is over, you're right back where you started in the same old pile of stinkin' thinkin'. I find it amazing that someone could criticize the concept of being motivated, even temporarily. Human motivation is a science. Within the confines of this science, there are varied opinions about what it takes to be motivated. Many opinions have validity, because what motivates people varies. Successful sports coaches understand that what may be a motivating factor for one person may be demoralizing for another. Some people need a pat on the back; others need a kick in the butt! Once you know what you're motivated by, you can then program yourself to get the kind of results you want from life.

Motivation won't let you do anything, but it will help you do everything better than negative thinking will!

—Zig Ziglar

Find What You Love to Do and Make a Career of It!

T he Bureau of Labor Statistics recently reported that 80 percent of the people working in today's labor force don't like what they do for a living. This is not a startling statistic. The fact that 66 percent of all heart attacks occur on Monday morning between the hours of 7:00 and 9:00 A.M. may demonstrate, in part, that many people work at jobs that make them sick.

We've been conditioned to go to school and get a job so that in some way, somehow, we will be fulfilled, at some point in the future. Unfortunately, for most people the future never happens the way they thought it would because they left it up to someone else. We cannot forget that we are ultimately responsible for our own happiness. That includes the joy we get from what we do for a living.

Few companies really maximize the potential of their people for competitive advantage. This is because so few people derive any real joy from the work they do. Only recently have colleges and universities begun to address the issues of entrepreneurship and work as an expression of who we are as people. Many people want to work for a cause above and beyond survival or monetary benefit.

You spend more than one-third of your life working; it makes sense to find something to do that gives you pleasure. Then why don't you? The answer might be fear! It's common for people to take the first job that comes along when they graduate from high school or college, rather than really analyzing their true interests and how to best utilize their skills. The pressure to survive—and the emphasis that's placed on finding a job as soon as possible—is immense. Some people think, "My dad is a doctor. His dad was a doctor. His dad was a doctor. Unless I want my dad to hate me, I'd better be a doctor."

We've all heard the stories about the premed or prelaw student with a secret desire to become an artist, or the banker who really wants to be a rock star. Because of pressures from others, however, they allow themselves to do something they really don't enjoy, even if they are well compensated. They don't realize that an erosion of their dreams started the day they compromised.

It will only be a matter of time before the true source of their motivation for life is launched to the forefront. It can take five, ten, fifteen, twenty, or even thirty years before a person asks themselves the question "Is this all there is to life?"

When we enjoy what we do for a living, it's much easier to be motivated, because motivation is driven from the inside out rather than the outside in. From that perspective, we have a greater measure of control over our emotions when our work reflects self-actualization and fulfillment rather than money or the continuous approval of others.

The Symptoms of Depression

Many people suffer from depression, which in many cases is brought about by a lack of motivation and meaning in their lives. Since we spend much of our waking day working, lack of satisfaction, challenge, or motivation at the workplace can be a major contributor to depression. If you have experienced four or more of the following symptoms for more than two weeks, you should seek a physical or psychological evaluation by a physician or mental-health specialist. The following feelings may be part of a normal grief reaction for someone who has recently experienced a loss. But professional treatment is warranted if the feelings persist with no improvement in mood, as this may indicate clinical depression.

- A persistent sad, anxious, or "empty" mood.
- Loss of interest or pleasure in ordinary activities.
- Decreased energy, fatigue, or feeling "slowed down."
- Sleep problems, such as insomnia, oversleeping, or early-morning awakening.
- Eating problems, such as loss of appetite or weight loss or gain.
- Difficulty concentrating, remembering, or making decisions.
- Irritability.
- Excessive crying.
- Recurring aches and pains that do not respond to treatment.
- Feelings of hopelessness or pessimism.
- Feelings of guilt, worthlessness, or helplessness.
- Thoughts of death or suicide or making a suicide attempt.*

I am not implying that every case of depression is brought about by someone's job; I'm merely saying it's true in many cases. The fact is that 80 percent of the people working don't like what they do. In many documented cases, this has led to depression.

*Source: National Institute of Mental Health Depression Awareness Program.

Overcome the Negative

I've been speaking professionally now for many years. There's nothing else that I'd rather do. I understand the old adage "Find something you love to do and you'll never have to work a day in your life." Everyone has something they are good at, something they can do better than anyone else and receive joy from at the same time. I admire people who excel at things that I'm not very good at, such as tennis, golf, nuclear science, physics, chemistry, art, record production . . . the list goes on and on.

Can you imagine jumping out of bed each morning with enthusiasm and vigor because you can't wait to get on with the day's activities? There are many people who do just that. I'm one of them. You can be, too!

As you think so shall you become.

—James Allen

Why is it that for every dreamer there's a doubter? For every visionary, a crowd of skeptics? It's human nature for some people to spend their lives bringing other people down. Negative thinking is one of the main reasons why many people fail in life. They look for all of the reasons why something won't work rather than why it will. With this mind-set, they're beat before the game even starts.

When acceptance of negative thinking sets in, you don't even have a chance. Whether you think you can or can't do something, you're right. Why do most people choose the negative? Because *we're born to win, but programmed to fail!* We are programmed into the negative from the beginning. By the time you reach the age of eighteen, you've heard the word *no* 200,000 times, seen 30,000 acts of violence, and had received more than 12 million messages in the form of advertising telling you how to look, what to eat, and how to feel.

These influences produce a negative self-image that will surely manifest itself into a negative person unless you break the pattern. Negative thinking is indicated by words and phrases such as "I can't," "It won't work," "We've always done it this way," and "Nobody in my family has ever become anything, so why even try?" And sometimes loving but misguided relatives tell us, "Just be a little more realistic,"

"Be reasonable," or "Don't get your hopes up too high!" Why should what they say or how they feel be a death sentence of mediocrity for you? I have discovered throughout the years that misery does love company. If you happen to find a dream strong enough to motivate you to accomplish something, it reminds some people of what they don't have the courage to do.

When my grandmother first took me in, many people, some in my own family, told her that I would only disappoint her, that I would never amount to anything, and that she was foolish to put hopes and dreams into me. What was worse was that I, an eleven-year-old kid, knew they were saying these things about me. But I decided that rather than let negative feedback put me down, I would use it as fuel to prove them wrong. Most of all, I used it to prove to myself that I was going to be somebody.

My grandmother used to always tell me to keep on believing in myself regardless of what other people thought. I ask you to do the same, no matter what other people might do or say. Keep on dreaming. Sometimes we can talk ourselves right out of something without even giving ourselves an opportunity to succeed! I remember playing football at the University of Minnesota against some of the top teams in the nation, such as Nebraska, Ohio State, and Michigan. It seemed that our coaching staff and the players were always in a state of panic when we played these teams. We approached these games in fear rather than with confidence, and this often resulted in us getting blown out of the stadium. We approached other teams differently in our preparation. When we competed against teams like Illinois, Iowa, and, of course, Northwestern, we believed we would win. And we did more often than not.

Always Play to Win

We were in Ann Arbor, Michigan, one Saturday to play the University of Michigan, ranked number two in the nation. The game was going to be on national television. The day before the game, as we went through our pregame drills, our head coach summoned all the players and asked us to look around the stadium. He told us to breathe in the atmosphere because the next day there would be 100,000 screaming jackasses in the stands. When Tony Dungy, who was our starting quarterback and happened to be from Michigan, informed the coach that his mother was coming to the game, the coach immediately changed the statement, saying that there would be 99,999 screaming jackasses in the stands. Well, it was business as usual. We expected to lose, and we did.

We were intimidated by the history and swagger of the big, bad Wolverines. We went into the game with the attitude that if we could just keep the score down and avoid too much embarrassment, we would gain a moral victory. Michigan had us down 35–0 at halftime. Guys on our team were pulling up lame and just plain quitting. In the fourth quarter, with a 46–0 lead in front of the entire nation on ABC, Bo Schembechler, the Michigan head coach, took a time-out with six seconds left, and then Michigan kicked a short field goal to make the score 49–0.

I can still remember our team walking off the field with our heads down, demoralized by all of the obnoxious fans and the shame that came from losing so badly. After the game, our coach walked across the field to inform Bo what a classless act it was to humiliate us so when the game was clearly out of reach. But the game was lost long before we took the field. It was lost in practice and in all of the meetings that had preceded the game. No one believed we could win that game, and we didn't. Were they 49 points better? They were because we thought they were. How many times have you stopped yourself cold from taking action on something that you wanted for yourself, simply because of fear? Winning is a state of mind. If you don't believe that you can succeed, you never will. Belief in yourself is powerful medicine and the starting point for all achievement.

So Close, but So Far

The ensuing year brought many unpleasant disappointments. We lost many games that would have allowed us to have an outstanding season and finished toward the middle of the pack with a 6–5 record, despite the fact that Tony Dungy led the Big Ten in passing and total offense.

We faced the top-ranked Wolverines of Michigan again in the seventh game of the season and lost a very tight game 27–21. After we fumbled inside of the Michigan twenty-yard line in the game's closing moments, the Wolverines recovered the fumble and ran out the clock, dashing all hopes of a 28–27 Minnesota upset. We believed in ourselves, but not enough to win the big one!

What Goes Around Comes Around

Because of our ineptitude, we were picked to finish next to last in the Big Ten conference the next year, ahead of the downtrodden Northwestern Wildcats. After struggling through our first seven games to a 4–3 record, we faced the mighty Michigan Wolverines again. They had a perfect 7–0 record and were ranked number one in the nation. We were 35-point underdogs, and for our seniors, myself included, this would be our last opportunity for redemption.

The week before we played the Wolverines, we had barely beaten Northwestern 7–3 at our homecoming, and the coach wanted to make some changes. He moved me from defensive end and started me at right offensive guard. Offensive linemen usually weigh 250 to 275 pounds, but I weighed a paltry 205. The coach felt we needed leadership on offense, and that I'd played the position in high school was a plus as far as he was concerned.

I practiced the entire week at that position with the idea that I would be pulling in and trapping the opposition. That week was a disaster. We were running around like Keystone Kops—unorganized, unpredictable, and scared. The Friday before the game we looked like F Troop, with guys jumping offside and making all kinds of errors. When the coach sent us in, I could see the look on his face. On top of that, I was to be playing across from players who were all–Big Ten and all-American: Defensive tackle Curtis Greer later played several years with the Cardinals; all-American linebacker Ron Simpkins went on to play for the Cincinnati Bengals. Who would have given me a chance against these guys, let alone our team against theirs? No one except us!

On game mornings we were always awakened by a call from the front desk and usually took a walk outside in the frigid Minnesota air. This was a home game at Memorial Stadium, which we called "the Brick House." After our walk, we ate, taped ankles and other joints, and held meetings by position. The night before, we had received one heck of a speech from George "Butch" Nash, one of our assistant coaches and a Minnesota football legend. He had told us to play like our lives were on the line; that for once in our lives, we should give it everything we had, and do our best, because that's all that anyone could ever expect of us. That morning, I kept remembering the sour taste in my mouth from the years before. I remembered how everyone cried in the locker room for bringing such shame to a once-proud University of

Minnesota football program. The seniors on our team made a vow to give it everything we had. We all kept saying, "Let it all hang out!"

On the bus, there was a buzzing sound in the air, an eerie feeling inside that told us something was going to be different. We didn't know what it was. When we went to the field, there were only about forty thousand fans in a stadium that held sixty-five thousand. But we felt like nothing mattered; the place could have been empty. We were playing for ourselves, regardless of the outcome.

Michigan kicked off, and we quickly drove sixty-five yards to score and take the lead, 7–0. During the touchdown play, I got whacked in the nose, and blood poured all over my jersey, pants, and face mask. But I knew one thing: Nobody was going to take me out of that game. This was our opportunity to have that one shining moment that everyone talks about. I wasn't about to be cheated out of it, blood or no blood.

The intensity after this drive was electric. The fans were going crazy, but everyone expected the mighty Wolverines to come back and put us in our gopher hole. The next thing they knew, it was halftime, and we had the lead 10–0. The stadium was a madhouse. We started the third quarter and found the stadium packed. People had been listening on the radio and decided to come to see if this was really happening. More than twenty-five thousand tickets were sold at halftime, and we were looking at the first packed house of the year. Michigan kicked off to us to start the second half. We drove the ball eighty yards without throwing a pass, then kicked a field goal. The score was 13–0.

When Michigan finally got the ball back, there was only 3:58 left in the third quarter. We were dominating the best college football team in the nation. Bo Schembechler, the coach who had so badly embarrassed us two years before, stared on in disbelief. We scored once more, with a field goal in the fourth quarter, to seal one of the biggest upsets in college football history: Minnesota 16, Michigan 0. It was the first time they'd been shut out in twenty-five years.

In the locker room after the game was over, there were lots of tears of joy and happiness. My coach came up to me, gave me a big bear hug, and with tears in his eyes said, "Son, you're what college football is all about!" That year, we defeated the University of Washington, which featured a quarterback named Warren Moon, and UCLA, which featured a host of superstars who would later go on to find fame in the NFL. We played in the Hall of Fame Bowl—the first bowl game that the university had gone to in more than sixteen years. Redemption at last!

We were basically the same guys who had been so miserable the year before. The difference was that we'd decided to move beyond the level of negative thinking that had held us back in the past and start believing in what was possible. We had nowhere to go but up.

Sometimes when people are the most desperate, they perform the best—as in the story of the ninety-pound woman who lifts a two-thousand-pound car off her child and then pulls the child to safety. Sports are an expression of the human condition. There are ups and downs, winning and losing, and situations that help people determine what kind of character they have within. I learned that day that I had every right to expect just as much success as anyone. So do you!

Don't ever let anyone turn you around on your dreams, because you never know what can happen. The incident with the Michigan game taught me how to be a winner. I've thought about that day many times when faced with other challenges. Think about times when you've accomplished something and really felt great about yourself. Capture the mood. What did the atmosphere feel like? What kinds of emotions were evoked from those feelings? Take those feelings, embrace them, remember them, and hold them always in the forefront of your mind to be recalled whenever you doubt yourself. The most powerful form of belief is self-belief. As Napoleon Hill once said, "Whatever the mind of man can conceive and believe, it can achieve!" I say *it will achieve*. If you don't achieve something, it's because deep down inside, you don't believe!

Many times we think that success happens only to other people. This mind-set guarantees failure. Do everything you can to eliminate negative thinking and negative people from your life. They will destroy your hopes and dreams if you allow them to. Beginning today, rededicate yourself to becoming better than you were yesterday. Renew any dreams that you may have placed on the back burner, and never, I mean never, think about giving up on *you!*

Regret

Many people suffer from regret because they don't have the courage to take action. They sit on the sidelines of life and take what's left after decisive people are finished. Many large companies have suffered from the wrath of regret. It doesn't matter how successful you may have been in the past, because the minute you think you've arrived, you're ready for the return trip back home.

Think about a powerful company like IBM. Just a few years ago they were held up as the pinnacle of corporate success. Other companies sent their people to IBM to find out what they were doing. Those people would go back home and do the same things with their companies. More often than not, they would work. IBM had figured out the combination to open the safe. Inside was massive success. Then, they rested too long and did not pay attention to what was happening in the marketplace. Meanwhile, it began to change.

Two guys out in Cupertino, California, Steve Jobs and Steve Wozniak, had a vision. They wanted to take huge mainframe computers the size of rooms, condense them, and place one in the hands of every person around the globe. They started a small company, and now their sales are in excess of $8 billion annually. It's Apple Computer! Before Apple Computer, certain assumptions were made, such as that hardware would always be the driving force behind the computer industry. Once-tiny Apple set IBM back on its heels.

"We shoulda," "We coulda," "If only we had," "Why didn't we think of that?" These comments often characterize regret. IBM made a tremendous comeback—the mark of a true champion—but much of the pain could have been eliminated had they paid more attention to detail and demanded more of themselves.

You and I must do the same if we are to reach our goals in life. That's the challenge of success. It's fleeting. That's why we must constantly seek to improve ourselves if we are going to stay ahead.

I spent several years with PepsiCo, Inc. It was always interesting to watch the dynamics between Pepsi and Coke. I felt like I was watching two twin brothers duke it out in a heavyweight fight. One throws a right; so does the other. One ducks; so does the other. They know each other's moves exactly. The only problem with that is they always wind up in the same place, in a dead heat: tied and continuing to argue about who's number one.

I felt like I was watching the old TV show and the question was, "Will the real number one please stand up?" At the beverage companies, it was, "No, we're number one!" "Wait a minute, we're number one!" Pepsi said, "We've got Michael Jackson!" Coke said, "We've got Michael Jordan!"

While Pepsi and Coke were arguing about who was number one, however, the marketplace changed. Baby Boomers began to become more health conscious and careful about everything that went into their bodies. They questioned whether or not drinking tons of water loaded with sugar and caffeine was good for them. They started making other choices and started drinking more teas, juices, and water.

Three window washers in upstate New York, Leonard Marsh, Hyman Golden, and Arnold Greenberg, were watching this trend. Instead of not doing anything out of fear, they asked the operative question, "How can we capitalize on the changes in the marketplace?" and created Snapple. They subsequently sold the company to Quaker Oats and became fabulously rich. Snapple sells more than $1 billion worth of its fruity tea drinks annually.

Meanwhile Pepsi and Coke found themselves lamenting, "We shoulda," "We coulda," "If only we had," "Why didn't we think of that?" Conventional thinking would say that there's no use in trying. Conventional thinking often leads to mediocrity. You've got to be able to see an opportunity and take action on it if you really want a chance to succeed.

After that, beverage-industry experts felt that the tea market was cornered, because not long after the Snapple miracle, Pepsi inked a multimillion-dollar deal with Lipton Tea. Coke countered with its own multimillion-dollar deal with Nestea. Many people thought it foolish to attempt to compete with these two industry giants without tons of cash for marketing.

Then Mike Schott brought out a new hit, Arizona iced tea. He didn't have a multimillion-dollar advertising budget, so he used a wild and very colorful twenty-four-ounce can. It leaped off of the shelves and captured the attention of the American consumer to the tune of more than $300 million a year.

Don't ever let anyone tell you what can't be done, because people are finding ways every day to do the seemingly impossible. The key is to find what you believe to be a good idea. As long as it's legal and does not violate the rights of your fellowman, go for it!

Excuses: Whatever You're Going to Do, Get On with It!

> *There are costs and risks to a program of action, but they are far less than the long range risks and costs of comfortable inaction.*
>
> **—John F. Kennedy**

It's amazing how many excuses people have for not taking action on their dreams. Some say, "I'm too young." Then, when they start to mature, they say, "I'm too old." You'll never be any younger. Each day that passes is one less you have to do what you want with your life. I gave a seminar in San Jose, California, not long ago. One of my participants was an eighty-five-year-old woman. She was vibrant and full of energy. When she shook my hand, she almost broke it! She didn't think she was too old. She had just bought a home and taken out a thirty-year mortgage. That's optimism! She was going back to college to get her degree because she had never gone to school. She was just starting another chapter of her life at a time when most people were waiting to die. She could have said, "Well, I'm going to wait until conditions change or get better." But she didn't have much time left.

While you might think that you have got lots of time, you don't have much time to play with either. I don't care if you're young—you don't wait for something to happen, you make something happen.

Many people suffer from the mañana syndrome: "I'll get around to that tomorrow"; "I'll do it some other time"; "I don't feel right about it right now." That happened to me not too long ago. My agent called me. We split up some duties, and I was supposed to call a couple of people. One of them was a person that I really didn't feel like talking to. I then thought to myself, "There is only right now!" I picked up the phone and called that person immediately. Most of us don't realize that when we decide not to do the major things that could improve our lives, we postpone our better future. This becomes a terrible pattern of behavior, and the older we get, the harder it is to take action and get the ball rolling.

I have a friend who always talks about what he wants to do but never follows up his dream with action. This friend was recruited to the University of Minnesota at the same time as myself, and we were both in the class of 1974. He never took school seriously, and he eventually flunked out. After that, he always seemed to have negative things to say about the university.

I've learned that a good friend is someone who won't allow you to dodge responsibility. They tell it like it is with you because they love you and want you to face what's real. Only then can you deal with the situation as it is and make the necessary changes to improve the situation. This comes from taking full responsibility for what happens to you.

I decided to be a real friend and tell it like it was. I told him he felt negatively about the university because he had unfinished business there. I suggested that he go back to school and complete his education. He said, "By the time I graduated from college, I would be forty-four years old!" I said, "How old are you going to be if you don't go?"

Now is the time to make things happen in your life. Pick a direction and go. Any one will do. Some people would ask, "What if it's the wrong direction?" My answer to that is always, "You'll find out more quickly! There's no substitute for action. If you make a mistake, you'll learn from it. If you succeed in your undertaking, it builds momentum and gives you confidence to try something else."

One of the key components for success is not just action, but *massive action!* The question is not, Can you do something? It is, Will you do it? Are you really willing to discipline yourself to take the actions necessary to expand your horizons by continuing your education, learning a new language, taking self-improvement classes, getting a license to sell real estate, putting together a new résumé, or making whatever changes are needed to improve the quality of your life? Are you willing to take charge of your life now and be responsible for your results?

That's how you eliminate the pain of regret. When you take action, win or lose, you set up in your mind that action is its own reward. When you act, you get a result and are given the formula for the next action, which could lead to larger possibilities.

Perhaps Charles Bernard Shaw said it best when he said, "People are always blaming their circumstances for what they are. I don't believe in circumstances. The people who get on in this world are the people who get up and look for the circumstances they want, and if they can't find them, they make them."

You must be willing to be accountable for your life. I've seen many broken men and women in my time. Many were alcoholics or drug addicts. As a youth, I was curious about why and how their lives turned out to be such tragedies. I watched beautiful young women and handsome young men with promising futures turn into outcasts. When I asked them about the reasons for their plight, it was always interesting that very few of them would actually take responsibility for their condition. There was always someone or something else to blame. Very few would step forward and say that they were the reason.

My little brother has been in and out of reform schools and correctional facilities all his life. I know that for many years he blamed me for running away from home, when I was eleven, and leaving him behind. He blamed my mother and father for the lives they led as young people. I agree that he got a raw deal as a kid. One night he called me from the state penitentiary at 1:30 A.M. and said he finally knew the reason he was in the joint. He said it was because of him. He admitted that even with the bad breaks he'd endured, he knew right from wrong.

I got down on my knees and thanked God. For the first time, I felt that he really had a chance at life because he was taking the first step to maturity and accountability for himself.

"If only I had!" "If only they wouldn't have!" "Had I not had so many bad breaks!" "If I had only gotten started when I was younger!" "I'm too young!" These are all the laments of the loser, the failure, the person who is never really willing to pay a price. I read a poem a few years ago that I often recall when thinking of these kinds of people.

> I bargained with life for a penny
> And life would pay no more
> However I begged at evening
> When I counted my scanty store
> You see, life is a just employer
> It will give you what you ask
> But once you have set the wages
> Why, then you must bear the task
> I worked for a menial's hire
> Only to find dismayed
> Any price I would have asked of life
> Life would have willingly paid
>
> **—Jessie B. Rittenhouse**

Winners vs. Losers

We can call a loser all kinds of things: helpless, pitiful, unsuccessful, an also-ran, enslaved, a lazy degenerate, "sorry," mediocre, and on and on. When someone says the word "winner," you automatically know what that means. You don't have to wonder, "What did they mean by that?" "Winner" has a ring to it, and you need not say more.

Winners aren't smarter, and they don't have any greater natural ability. Most winners have one simple ability: the ability to decide what they want and to take the actions necessary to make it happen. It's all a matter of choice, not chance!

Other species must depend solely on the instinct to survive. That's not true with people; we can make something out of nothing. We can turn pennies into fortunes, or take the most dire circumstances and transform our lives into successes, creating opportunity for others in the process. We all have an obligation to leave this world in a little bit better condition than we found it. The true test of a successful life is not how long we live but how we live. When we seek to contribute to a greater cause than ourselves, it is virtually impossible for us not to benefit in the process.

> *Life means to have something definite to do—a mission to fulfill—and in the measure in which we avoid setting our life to something, we make it empty. Human life, by its very nature, has to be dedicated to something.*
>
> **—José Ortega y Gasset**

Living with "I Can and I Will"

The future belongs to those of us who know and perform. The highest level of thinking is called integration. It says, *I can! I will!* and *I must!* achieve success; it is my birthright to maximize my potential and become the best person I possibly can. In my estimation, this type of thinking comes when you are truly attuned to who you are as a person, what your chief aim in life is, and what price you are willing to pay to make your dreams come true.

The majority of today's corporations operate with a mission statement. This is a declaration of the direction of the organization. It is posted throughout the company as a reminder of what the company stands for. I believe our lives are the same way. If someone were to ask you for your personal mission statement in life, would you be able to give them one? Without one, it will be difficult for you to remain consistent in your values, actions, and results.

My Mission Statement: To aid individuals in personal development and growth by offering information, ideas, and solutions that help them achieve measurable results in a reasonable time as they strive to achieve excellence in all areas of their personal and professional lives.

Your mission statement differs from your purpose statement in that it focuses on what you want to give. The purpose statement should be focused on what you would like to become or do. I suggest that you find a quiet place and write a mission statement that reflects what you would like to do with your life. Your mission may change, depending upon your situation at a given point in time. For example, a couple trying to raise three children may have different individual mission statements before the children are grown and have moved out than they would have afterward.

As your situation and priorities change, it is possible for your mission statement to change. The key thing is to take the time to think about your life without waking up every day as a creature of reaction and habit. You will be surprised at the clarity and sense of purpose you will have after completing this exercise. You will feel much freer and in control of your destiny. After you have penned your mission, place it somewhere so you can see it often. It will remind you of why you're doing what you're doing when your dobber is down and you have cause to question yourself.

As we strive to achieve this level of integration, we may need to tune in to everything that happens to us and use it to realize our mission in life. Every New Year's Eve, CNN runs a special report that reviews the lives of famous people who have died that year. I often marvel at some of the accomplishments of these people. Most of them have achieved excellence in their fields, while others have become infamous rather than famous.

The one thing that sticks in my mind from this show is that regardless of their accomplishments, these people are no longer with us. They're dead.

Each of us is given a finite amount of time on this spinning planet. No one of us knows when the last grain of sand in the hourglass will fall and the game will end. We will gain deeper insight and appreciation for life if we allow the power of reflection and introspection to work for us.

In St. Louis, I played football and basketball against a great athlete, Randy Frisch. He went to Vianney High School, a rival of Christian Brothers Military High School, where I went. Randy was big and scrappy with curly red hair. He stood about six feet, five inches and weighed in at around 275. He was known as a bully. He was a stud on the football field and a brute on the basketball court.

When I first laid eyes on Randy, I didn't like him. As it turned out, my perception of him was all wrong. Even though he carried himself with a swagger, I learned it was more out of confidence than arrogance. He was a good guy, but with a mean streak if you got on the wrong side of him. I saw his mean side on several occasions when people gave him a hard time in public. They would soon learn he was no one to fool with, but he would never provoke anything himself.

Over the course of the next few years, we became good friends. He went on to the University of Missouri on athletic scholarship. One year later, I graduated from high school and enrolled at the University of Minnesota. We continued to work out together through the summers. We lifted weights at the same club and ran together in that humid Missouri heat to the point of almost passing out. I really loved this guy!

During Randy's senior year, his team was awesome. Mizzou upset Alabama in their home opener and went on to beat Nebraska and three other teams ranked in the top ten. Randy was a defensive tackle and had a great year. Later, he was drafted by the Pittsburgh Steelers and was doing well in training camp. He was slated to play behind Mean Joe Greene on the most dominant defense ever assembled in professional football.

We were all proud of Randy and were looking forward to seeing him play in the fall. He and I had just completed our final summer workout only three weeks before I got the good news from Tony Dungy, who was also at training camp, about how well Randy boy was doing. Tony said Randy was going to make the team. The following week, the Pittsburgh Steelers faced off against the Philadelphia Eagles in a preseason game. Randy played very well.

I got a phone call at 7:30 the next morning as I was preparing to leave St. Louis to report to Minneapolis for my senior year. It was Randy's mother. She was crying so hard, I could feel the pain as if I were there in person. After the game, Randy was driving back from the team's practice facility in Latrobe, Pennsylvania, when an oncoming truck swerved and hit him head-on. He was killed instantly. I couldn't believe my buddy was dead.

I hung up the phone, walked out onto the front porch, and collapsed in a chair and cried for hours. I kept remembering working out and hanging out together, thinking of the brotherhood we had established.

My grandmother stepped out to the porch and asked me to come inside. She sat in a large living-room chair, and I sat down in the same chair with my head resting on her lap and cried some more. I asked her why God had let me live but had taken Randy away when he had so much to look forward to. He was about to live out a childhood dream. The same one I had, along with so many other kids. Nonnie explained that God has plans for all of us but sometimes chooses to use us in different ways, ways we sometimes don't understand. She told me to learn from all of the things Randy and I did together and to remember that each day is not promised to any of us. She said that I should observe and learn how to take the things that happen in life and use them to become a better person.

I learned that as long as we are here on earth, God has a purpose for us. That purpose is to contribute to the betterment of the world. Why not take advantage of life now? Why wait until something drastic happens in order to get yourself to move off the mark?

You must learn to love yourself. I'll never forget that summer day when I got the news about Randy. I promised then I would make something of my life. I looked up and down my block, and one thing hit me squarely between the eyes: Most of the kids my age were dead! I wanted to make something of myself for those who had never had a chance—Robbie, Greg, Jewell, Terrance, Keith, Sandra, Preston, John, Roni, Lamont, Norvell, Reggie, Larry, Alvin, and all the others who never saw their twenty-first birthdays. Bring to the forefront all of the lessons of life and use them to live with a greater sense of passion, purpose, commitment, and meaning.

CHAPTER 3
THE POWER OF SELF-ESTEEM
(YOU AND YOUR INNER DIALOGUE)

Endure

*A wise woman had an inspiring story
she would sometimes tell, about a
young lass with eyes of light and
beauty fancied by every male.*

*She claimed that with every year that
came to pass, nothing blemished the
beauty of this bright-eyed lass.*

*When asked by the town hags,
"What manner of woman is thee?"
The lass replied, "The beauty you envy
endures because of that inside me.*

*"The secret is to harbor no jealousy,
hatred, or envious fear, that goodness
and laughter fill you with youth
each passing year."*

*Beauty, more than skin deep, lasts
according to the attitude you keep!*

—Saunni Dais

> *To be nobody but yourself in a world which is doing its best, night and day, to make you everybody else means to fight the hardest battle which any human being can fight; and never stop fighting.*
>
> **—E. E. Cummings**

We live in a society that stresses the importance of looking youthful and taking care of our physical health. People spend millions of dollars on health-club memberships, spas, and vitamins. At the same time, we pay little attention to our mental health. A huge part of your mental health is your self-esteem. How you feel about yourself will determine the quality of your life and the results you get from it. Many of us have low self-esteem because of our past. Sometimes it can take us years to come to terms with those demons and move on to the better future we deserve.

You are conditioned to feel the way you do about yourself. From the day you are born, you are given feedback by your parents, your relatives, and the outside world. From this feedback you form an opinion of yourself. You should always be aware of the impact and influence you may have on another person. Whether you realize it or not, somebody is watching.

I Didn't Make You Up!

My little sister, Kumonte, was born from a marriage of my mother's after my father and she were divorced. When I ran away from home, my sister was just a baby. Over the next twenty-five years I saw her a handful of times. We talked on the phone once or twice. It was at a wedding in Los Angeles that we had a chance to really get to know each other. When we saw each other there, she ran into my arms with tears streaming down her face, saying to everyone in earshot, "Hey, this is my brother! This is my big brother, you all!" She whispered into my ear that throughout the years, when she told people she had a big brother, they thought she was lying. "They thought I made you up because they never saw you!" she said. She then looked around, shouting with joy, "I told you I had a brother, and here he is!"

She told me she had been waiting for this moment for years. I was floored to think of the influence I'd had without ever being around. This taught me a valuable lesson about the power of influence and the effect one person can have on our lives. It starts from the moment we enter this world. Everything you come in contact with leaves its stamp on you. Self-esteem, like motivation, is a matter of conditioning. Just as physical conditioning is critical to health, so good self-esteem is critical to mental health.

Mental Mastery: Four Levels of Mental Competency

We've all heard about the concept of mental conditioning, but few people purposely seek it. Unless you make a concerted effort each day to question the information that comes into your world, you could very well open your mind up to things that aren't necessarily in your best interest. Many times, it seems, we are on automatic pilot, reacting to the things that happen to us rather than operating from a position of control. There are four basic levels of competency:

Level One: Unconscious Incompetence

This mental condition is one of ignorance of skills and potential. People who have it are content to just get by. They know their personal development is deficient, and they don't care. This kind of thinking is a recipe for disaster, no matter how successful you have been in the past. Everything is changing, and the bar for success continues to rise. Many people get frustrated because the skills that were necessary for success in the past are obsolete today, but that's part of progress. They need to sharpen their attitude toward learning and start to take advantage of change.

Level Two: Conscious Incompetence

At this stage, you know you are incompetent and that your skill level does not match the things you want for yourself in life. You become willing to take those first steps toward education or reeducation to afford yourself the opportunities new skills could attract. Many times you will find you must sacrifice old methods of behavior that had you trapped at the Unconscious Incompetence level; for instance, you might forgo sitting at home watching the sports channel in order to take a class in the evening to learn computer skills. This approach works no matter what the endeavor. The person frustrated by poor golf scores or the inability to swim who decides to take lessons and then improves increases their self-esteem in the bargain.

Level Three: Conscious Competence

At this level you begin to gain some skills, but you don't feel fully confident about what you're doing. It takes all of your energy and focus to pull something off. Remember when you first learned to ride a bicycle, while the training wheels were still on? Each time you pedaled, the bike got wobbly, your body shook, and you tried to maintain control. You were at a level where you knew what to do but had not developed the skill to master it. This is the beginning of growth and personal development, providing you don't stop exploring. At this point, you must constantly dedicate and rededicate yourself to learning everything you can about what interests you.

Level Four: Unconscious Competence

This is the highest level of mental conditioning. You feel so confident that you don't even have to think about it. Mental confidence has become a reflex. If someone were to blindfold you, take you to your house, and tell you that if you could successfully operate with a blindfold on, you would win $10,000, do you think you could do it? If nothing was moved from its normal place, chances are you could. You know exactly where things are: the toothbrush, your sock drawer, the distance from the bedroom to the bathroom. You can see the hallway in your mind's eye, and you know exactly how many steps are necessary to get there. You are unconsciously competent.

Have you noticed that after you've owned the same car for a while, you no longer have to look at the ignition in order to insert the key? You are on automatic pilot. Your hand simply guides the key into the ignition while you are yelling out the window for your kids to clean up their rooms. The car starts while your attention is focused on a million other things. You are unconsciously competent. You can achieve this level of mastery in anything you choose if you're willing to work at it. This comes from a commitment to continue to practice, drill, and rehearse at something until it becomes second nature. When this happens, you can operate with a great degree of control.

You're Born to Succeed,
but Programmed to Fail

What if you invited me over to your house and I brought a huge barrel of trash and dumped it all over your living-room floor? Would you be upset with me? Most likely not only would you be enraged, but you would probably also toss me out on my rump! Why is it we let people dump trash into our minds and never question it? Some of the things we read, listen to, and watch are bleeding us of our possibilities one pinprick at a time. We don't even question it, yet we wonder why we don't get the kinds of results we want.

When I was a kid, I had an unlimited imagination. I would dream about being everything I thought I wanted to be—an astronaut one day, a rock 'n' roll singer the next. The only limits at that time were my ability to dream. What happened? I came in contact with a system that's supposed to educate me, right?

So often we learn about the limitations of human potential rather than the possibilities. We are taught from an early age not to run into the street or we'll get run over, to have our feet firmly planted on the ground, to be realistic about our potential, and to be practical in our approach. When I was in college, some professors would come in on the first day of class and tell us how many people would receive A's, B's, C's, and F's. It was amazing how close they were in their forecasts. This alone should have told them something! It is human nature for people to rise to the level of expectation others have for them.

When I was a baby, there was a lady who used to baby-sit for me, Miss Hayes. She was a wonderful woman. I remember her changing my diapers and telling me how pretty, smart, and capable I was. She would comment, "One day you're going to set the world on fire!" I've remembered this woman my entire life, even though she has been dead for thirty years and I haven't seen her since I was seven years old.

It's amazing what happens when you instill positive messages into the minds of others. It can have a lifelong effect. I think of Miss Hayes often when dealing with my own children, and I try to give them that special gift Miss Hayes gave me: a feeling of self-worth. Miss Hayes was a wise woman. I will be forever grateful to her for her kindness and warmth.

A Mountain of a Woman

My eighth-grade teacher, Vernice Bates, was a wonderful woman. Miss Bates stood six feet tall and dressed impeccably. She was an excellent teacher who didn't take guff from anyone. I went to a very tough elementary school, known for its share of thugs and hoodlums. It was different when they came into Miss Bates's class. She told us up front that we were bright, capable students and that she was going to push us to reach our full potential. She let us know what was expected of us and said she would see to it that we "walked the line." She had a large yardstick covered from top to bottom with duct tape. When you got out of line, you knew it was more than geography you were going to learn.

One afternoon, one of the kids in class was becoming disruptive. Miss Bates brought out the yardstick and immediately took control of the class. She told the girl to bend over and look to the east, and she gave the girl three swats on the backside. The next day, the girl's mother stormed into class reading Miss Bates the riot act. Miss Bates told the child to get her coat and then had the principal escort the mother and her child out. Miss Bates informed the child's mother that she was the boss; if the girl's mother didn't like it, she could keep her daughter at home and teach her herself. Two days later the mother came back with the child, pleading with Miss Bates to allow the child to return. She vowed that she would support Miss Bates any way she could to see that her child behaved herself and did her classwork.

As strict as Miss Bates was, she was very kind and loved her students. She didn't believe in the concept of helplessness! She held us accountable for our behavior and let us know when we were falling short. Her classes were known for learning and discipline.

To this day, whenever I come across people with whom I've attended elementary school, we cannot have a conversation without one of us mentioning Miss Bates. She had high expectations for her students, strict standards of behavior, and the courage to stand up for what was right. She programmed us to win. Each day she told us she had big hopes and dreams for us and that we should always see ourselves doing great things. Many of the students, including myself, took her words of encouragement to heart.

Our Mental Programming and the Media: You Have the Power to Choose

Behavioral scientists tell us that more than 75 percent of all of the thoughts that come into our minds are negative. Imagine how most Americans start their day: They awaken to the morning news, filled with reports of tragedies from the previous day. They augment that with a dose of the daily newspaper, filled with reports of muggings, murders, rapes, high interest rates, inflation, higher taxes, increased debt, deaths, and bankruptcies. Then they go to work at a job they probably hate or feel indifferent about.

This sounds pretty bleak, doesn't it? Well, it doesn't have to be that way. Can you imagine loading up on all of that negative programming and then attempting to have a rich, dynamic life? It can't be done! You must learn to control the information that comes into your mind so that you don't get overburdened with programming that could destroy your positive outlook.

I came down with the flu one time and was so sick I couldn't get out of bed. You've been there. You wake up and your mind says, "Let's go out there and make things happen." But your body says, "Hey, fool, I'm sick. What are you trying to do, kill me?"

I made the worst mistake. I turned on daytime television to keep me company. I'm usually not much of a television watcher, especially during the daytime—I'm too busy. In the background there was Ricki Lake, Sally Jesse Raphael, Jerry Springer, Montel Williams, Jenny Jones, and so on. I heard about rape and incest, mothers sleeping with their daughters' boyfriends, fathers dating their daughters' boyfriends, murder, and bizarre stories that depicted the lowest human behavior.

If I was ill at 8:30 in the morning, by the time 5:30 P.M. arrived, emotionally speaking, I was ready for intensive care. I asked myself why the American public was so enamored with the sensational, the negative, and the hideousness of failure, and I came up with this: We are programmed to be excited about the negative. It makes people who don't have the desire or the courage to take a stand and think for themselves feel better. It requires little thought, very little energy, and no creativity.

The key thing to understand is that you and I control exactly what we choose to focus on at any moment in our lives. If you believe this, you have the ability to select the ingredients that create the fabric of your thoughts, which control your actions and guide your destiny. I'm not advocating that you throw out your television and never read the newspaper—although for some, that wouldn't be a bad idea. I'm suggesting that you guard against overloading your mind with negative input. You have to see to it that you are mentally healthy. No one cares as much as you should. When we allow ourselves to be influenced by this kind of programming, it teaches us dependency, and trains our minds to look for excuses rather than solutions.

Check Yourself

With two small children of my own, I understand more deeply each day how their mental outlook on life depends on the example I set—more by what I do than what I say. I notice that when I'm working on a difficult task and they're watching, it is critical that I handle frustration in a way that teaches them patience and resiliency. It is shocking to notice how they will respond just as I do when faced with their own little challenges. If they see me react impatiently when doing something, I will later see that behavior in them.

What if each day you were told how bright, beautiful, smart, capable, loving, kind, and needed you were? How do you think that would make you feel? Do you think you would have a different mental picture of yourself than if you were constantly told what a horrible person you were? Absolutely! That's why what we pay attention to is so critical to how we feel about ourselves and the world around us. Your self-concept determines whether you have impotent goals or ones that empower you. You can only have large goals to the extent that you see yourself capable and worthy of those goals. For that reason, how you think about yourself determines what actions you are willing to take. Your life will manifest these thoughts.

To many people, the concept of consciously thinking about and projecting a larger image of themselves is silly. They leave it up to someone or something else. What you focus on is what you get. You must make sure there are more positive than negative stimuli going into your head. There are so many wonderful things happening in the world.

I believe that for every negative thing that happens, there are a thousand positive things. It's how things get done! That's how bridges get built, curriculums get created, and things that improve the quality of our lives get invented. This is one of the most exciting times to be alive. We have more technology, more opportunities, more information, and more assistance than ever before. They key is to understand that success is not in short supply. Remember, there's plenty of prosperity to go around. You just have to be willing to stake your claim.

You Attract What You Think About

I'll never forget an experience I had with a group of guys I used to play basketball with a few years ago. We would shoot hoops for two or three hours at a time. Afterward, we'd gather at someone's house to play cards, drink beer, and solve all of the world's problems. We spent hours wasting time. It seemed that for most of the guys there, this was the closest thing to real work they encountered.

This went on every day, and I usually participated when I wasn't on the road doing my job. One day it hit me. I started to think about each guy in the room, fifteen altogether. When I took inventory of this group, I was the only guy in the room with a job. I started to panic; my heart started to pound. I thought to myself, "I've got to get out of here!" These were not bad guys; they just weren't highly motivated.

I wanted more from life than just talking about the conditions of life; I wanted to create them. As I thought about it, I realized I had attracted these guys through my own passive outlook. I also realized that in order to attract people I could learn from, I would have to raise my standards. Most of us were from the inner city, products of dysfunctional families, poverty, drugs, and violence. We always talked about how bad the conditions were and how awful the system was. No solutions, just problems.

Finally I said, "I'm sick and tired of always hearing about the negative in terms of what can't be done! Why don't we do something about it?

Things aren't going to change by us just sitting here talking about the same things we talk about every time."

As I stormed out the door, I felt mixed emotions. I felt vindication; maybe, I thought, I had cut through some of the mental clutter. At the same time, I felt remorse because maybe I had alienated guys I had known for years. I got a call later that evening from the friend at whose house we'd gathered. He said a spirited debate had taken place after I'd left, and everyone had agreed that we were on a slow boat to nowhere. The group broke up shortly thereafter. Maybe that's the best thing that could have happened.

What You Say to Yourself

Self-talk is what you say to yourself and about yourself. It affects your self-image. Your self-image is the accumulation of all of your attitudes about your chances of success or failure. This has a great deal to do with your performance, as well as your willingness to try something again if you do not at first succeed. If you succeed at something, your self-talk tells you that you are good at the particular thing and that perhaps it comes easily for you. You may find yourself saying, "It's just like me to do that" or "You know, I've always been that way." When you make comments such as this, you reinforce a positive self-image. This also gives you the confidence to speak positively to yourself in the future when faced with the same task. This creates a positive core belief system and a sense of certainty about possible outcomes.

We can create positive self-talk by the use of affirmations (internal, cognitive statements that establish a specific course, direction, outcome, or state of being for the future). "Affirmation" means to ratify or confirm something to be true. Some examples of positive affirmations are as follows:

I am worthy of success!

Each day, in every way, I'm getting better and better!

I am a smart, capable person!

I have tons of personal energy!

I enjoy helping other people!

I will succeed in my goals no matter how long it takes!

I will become the best person I can be!

I deserve success!

I am emotionally strong!

I love my life!

I am healthy and vibrant!

I am not getting older, I'm getting better!

I'm outgoing when I want to be!

Every day is my day if I make it that way!

The only way I can fail is if I quit!

I get along with all kinds of people!

I respect and value people who are different from me!

This list is obviously not all-inclusive, but just imagine what each day would be like if you told yourself these things and reinforced them. What do you think your chances to develop a more positive self-image would be? I suggest you take time to write positive affirmations regarding anything you want to do in life. For example, I had many challenges finding the courage to sit down and write this book. Even though I had been successful as a businessman and a professional speaker, I had never written a book. One of the things I did was to write affirmations about my goal of being an author. Here's what I came up with.

Goal: To write a self-help book that will empower others to take control of their lives and realize their dreams by unleashing the greatness within them.

Affirmations:

I am a good writer!

I will not quit until this book is written!

I am committed to this undertaking!

There are people who need my help!

I have an obligation to serve my fellowman!

I will deliver the best possible product!

This book will teach me about myself!

I am worthy of this book's success!

I am an effective and efficient writer!

I am a man of action!

Notice that I've placed exclamation points at the end of each statement, because how you say something is important. This is also true in self-talk.

The Three Components of Communication

1. Words: 7 percent

2. Voice quality (tone and pace): 38 percent

3. Physiology: 55 percent

You can see that 93 percent of communication is not what we say but how we say it. If I walked into a room and saw that you were upset about something, I could ask, "What's wrong with you?" or I could ask, "What's troubling you?" How I communicated the question would affect your response and how you felt from that point forward.

Make sure you speak with excitement about your affirmations. Make sure that from now on, when someone asks you how things are going, you tell them, *Great!* If you can't bring yourself to say that, then simply say, *Unbelievable!* That way you're covered no matter how things are going. How we use our bodies also plays an important role in helping us form positive self-images. From this moment on, walk with your back straight and your head up. Carry yourself as if you have already achieved your dream.

I Am the Greatest!

After Muhammad Ali captured the Olympic gold medal in 1960, he began a quest to become the heavyweight boxing champion of the world. Many thought he was an arrogant blowhard. But Ali was a great athlete, not only because he had great skill (he could "float like a butterfly and sting like a bee") but also because he was a master at psychology.

When Ali proclaimed he was the greatest of all time, Sonny Liston was still the heavyweight champion. Ali did such a masterful job of public relations that people started to tag him with the label "the Greatest" long before he defeated Liston and captured the crown.

Before the fateful fight with Liston, Ali stood in the locker room with his right-hand man, Drew "Bundini" Brown. As Ali warmed up, Bundini repeated over and over, "You're the greatest!" "You're the man!" "Women love you!" "Children love you!" "You're the champ!" and "You're so pretty!" By the time Ali got into the ring, he was worked up into such a frenzy that he was far more mentally prepared for the fight than Liston was. That combined with his God-given ability made him an unbeatable competitor.

Ali was a master of self-talk! The proclaimed "Louisville Lip" talked and performed himself into being one of the most recognized public figures ever. He also, more often than not, psyched his opponents right out of their minds. Many were stronger men with greater punching power, but Ali's mental games were dominant. The majority of his opponents were beaten long before the first round—they, too, believed he was the greatest. Without any formal training, Ali was demonstrating the skills and methods of affirmation and self-talk. For him they came naturally.

Using Affirmations

There are some important principles to keep in mind in order to derive the greatest benefits from affirmations. First, you must *read* the words aloud. This will trigger your subconscious to take command. The subconscious mind cannot distinguish between the false and the real. So the commands you give it are what it has to work with.

The second thing is to *visualize* and see yourself performing the task down to the most finite details. The more detailed and clearer the picture, the greater the effect on your subconscious mind. As you read the affirmations to yourself, imagine yourself crossing the finish line with arms raised, fully achieving the goal of your choice. See this vision in living color, as though you were watching a movie. See it in slow motion, in fast speed, and at every possible angle.

Allow yourself next to *emotionalize* as you accomplish your goal. What does the atmosphere look like? How does it feel? Who else is involved? In writing your affirmations, it's also important to:

1. Write them in the first person.

2. Write them in the present tense, as though they are already true and a part of your life at this moment.

3. Write them using emotional words that clearly describe the mental picture you see of yourself reaching your goal.

After writing your affirmations, spend at least thirty minutes or more a day, preferably early in the morning or before you retire for the evening, saying, picturing, and feeling your affirmations. I often use music, usually New Age or soft jazz without lyrics. This helps me create a theme for my affirmations. There are several songs I can simply listen to and they will automatically bring to my mind my affirmations, goals, or visions.

I also strongly suggest that you record your affirmations and listen to them often. This will again embed these positive messages in your mind. Remember, there is an entire series of actions that must be taken.

Reading: Just reading your affirmations will have only a 10 percent impact on your subconscious mind, limiting the results you get from the process.

Reading and Visualizing: This will anchor your subconscious mind further and allow you to achieve a 55 percent impact on your subconscious mind.

Reading, Visualizing, and Emotionalizing: This will allow you to affect your subconscious mind 100 percent so that you can reach your goals more quickly, enjoying the process as you succeed.

There are a couple of things I need to say about negativity. The first is that negative thoughts, occurrences, and experiences are normal. I didn't say they are good; negative things are not a major component of success, but they are something we must acknowledge.

Second, just as you can tell yourself what a wonderful person you are, you can also beat yourself up and analyze all of your worst qualities. In the section on negative thinking, you learned how a person's mind can be programmed negatively, so from this point forward, we are going to focus on solutions. The solutions come from your own ability to give yourself permission to believe in yourself.

Do Something Different

It's amazing what a fresh, new approach can do for us. So change yours. Break your old patterns of doing things and try something new. Try coming home and not turning on the television. Just enjoy the silence of your own company.

If you have a family, try to enjoy an evening with them without interference from outside influences. Turn off the TV! (When that happens, people begin to communicate with each other.) If you're used to lumbering out of bed in just enough time to do everything but are always running ten minutes behind, get up an hour earlier. Believe me, the trade-off in extra sleep is not worth the stress of feeling constantly overwhelmed. When you do something different from the norm, you'll notice things you didn't before and discover things that will afford you the opportunity to learn more about yourself. These distinctions will give you a new lease on life.

One of the things I enjoy as a diversion is sneaking into the movies during the middle of the afternoon. If I happen to drive by a theater and a movie is starting, I will dart in there for a couple of hours and escape the pressures of the day. Another favorite diversion of mine is going into a bookstore and getting lost in different books. I read, which is a form of entertainment for me, and I learn a great deal at the same time. I get dual benefits from the same activity. I usually leave with a half dozen books to add to my library, so the bookstore benefits as well.

You will find that no matter what the conditions are, successful people are doing something differently from unsuccessful ones. When tax laws change, successful people don't complain about it; they take classes to learn how to benefit from the new system. If interest rates go up, they find other, creative ways to finance their ventures. They don't sit around waiting for things to get back to the way they used to be.

Back in 1982, when I started my real estate business, people told me it was the wrong time to buy property because interest rates were 11 percent. They said I would never be able to charge enough rent to service the debt. Since then, I've bought and sold real estate worth more than $3 million and have become financially independent. What's even more exciting is I'm just getting started. I simply did something different from the people who were stifled by conditions. I used creative financing and found better and more profitable uses for properties.

For some reason, many people look at the walls of life as permanent. You must take detours, sometimes right in the middle of your designated course, in order to reach your destination. I suggest that you search for alternate routes ahead of time, so that when you get sidetracked, you've thought about the detours in advance. This will provide you with more options.

CHAPTER 4
YOUR POWER TO CHOOSE

*Your "experiences" are the evidence
that your Esteem and Dreams are
Pygmalion to your day to day. Desire
sires fire required to lift yourself higher.
The "I-fulfilling Prophecy"
will build your most passionate,
emotional, and recurring desires.*

*If your mind can conceive, then your
heart believes, and that's what
your spirit retrieves.*

*Your Will shall read and deliver every
message. It shall clear the way for
your desire's passage. When the Will
and Belief pair and bear fruit as one,
sweet or sour, you'll embrace what
your Will has done.*

—Saunni Dais

> *The person who is tenacious of purpose in a rightful cause is not shaken from their firm resolve by the frenzy of their fellow citizens clamoring for what is wrong or by the tyrant's threatening countenance.*
>
> **—Horace**

Sometimes we've got to be willing to make difficult, unpopular decisions. This often involves people whose effect on us is negative. When I was younger, I had a friend named Greg. We did everything together. We loved sports and often would play baseball, basketball, and football all in the same day. He was an excellent athlete. We had dreams of one day going to college and making it big. But Greg had one weakness: He was always attracted to people who had a negative influence on him. As long as he was away from these guys, he was fine. Unfortunately, he often found himself having to choose between doing what he knew was right and doing the wrong things in order to be accepted by a group of thugs.

I decided at this point that I could no longer associate with him. I knew that many of these guys around him were bad news. Most of them had criminal records, and many of them never saw their twentieth birthdays. Greg eventually got involved in selling heroin.

It broke my heart when I came home from college for a break to find that Greg was dead. He had been shot in the head at point-blank range in a house down the street from where we both lived. I thought about how easy it would have been for me to be lying in that funeral home instead of him. Letting go of people who negatively influence our lives is always a difficult and often an unpleasant choice to make.

A woman at a seminar once asked me, "What do you do if you have negative relatives in your family?" I told her to love them from a distance! Yes, sometimes people in your own family can be the worst at lowering your self-esteem. Sometimes they mean well in telling you not to expect too much or not to get your hopes up too high. What they don't understand is that through their own ignorance, they are ruining your chances for success. They failed because they gave up. Now they are asking you not to try.

Learn to Program Your Own Mind

The human brain is the most powerful computer on earth. You must learn to think for yourself without letting the programming from outside influences determine your outcome. It's a personal choice. You must learn to run your own mental PC. What a great metaphor the computer is for how our brain works. It has three basic components—the screen, the keyboard, and the disk—that must operate in tandem in order for it to function effectively, just as the human brain has many parts that must function together for you to operate at peak efficiency.

The Screen

The screen is a great metaphor for your behavior. I want you to imagine you're watching a movie on your computer screen. You are the star of the show. The next time you think about your life, ask yourself a question: "Is my behavior congruent with the things I want out of life?" Do you like what you see? If you don't, know that you have the power to change it. How do you treat others? Is a situation better or worse because you are involved? Are you a positive force or a negative one? Are you part of the solution or part of the problem? If your life is not what you want it to be, why isn't it? Are you willing to do what it takes to change for the better?

Many people want things out of life, but they don't have the discipline to make themselves do what it takes to get them. They want to make more money, but they do not develop themselves so that they are worthy enough to earn it. They want better health, but instead of joining a health club or jogging after work, they resort to doing the same old things that got them to the unhappy place they now occupy. You must understand that you can make a difference in this world. It is your obligation to do so. Will you be the next person to step forward and make a difference?

If we made an honest appraisal of ourselves, most of us would admit we could do much more and become much more than we currently are. It's a fact that most of us only use about 10 percent of our brain capacity. Some people even brag about it, as if to say, "Hey, look at me! I'm only using ten percent of my ability!" I believe that one of the real keys to happiness is the feeling you get from constantly growing and helping someone else do the same. You have the power in your hands to make a difference; never underestimate the power you have within you to influence someone and make a difference. Someone is watching. You may not even be aware of it. Maybe they're your kids or other relatives. Maybe it's a close or distant friend. It could even be a total stranger who is looking for some answers to life's challenges. Maybe it's someone on the verge of suicide who finds a ray of hope through watching something you do or say. Whether you know it or not, somebody's watching!

Teddy Stollard was a boy you would have labeled as least likely to succeed. He often reported to school with uncombed hair, wearing musty old clothes. He appeared to be anything but a model student. In class, he could often be seen staring out into space. When his fourth-grade teacher, Miss Thompson, asked him a question, he would respond by mumbling back to her in monosyllables. He was unattractive, unmotivated, and distant.

Even though Miss Thompson said she loved and treated all of her students the same, deep down inside, she knew this wasn't true. She treated Teddy differently, and she knew it! She often got a kind of perverse pleasure out of placing large red X's next to his wrong answers on tests. Whenever she gave him an F, she did it with a bit of a flair, writing the F at the top of the page with a big red felt pen.

She should have known better; she had his records. All the information on him was right there. They showed that Teddy had demonstrated promise with his work and attitude in first grade but had a poor home situation. In second grade, Teddy began showing signs of slowness. His mother was very ill. He received little encouragement from home. His mother died that year. In third grade, Teddy was a good boy but very reserved. He was much too serious for a child so young. In fourth grade, Teddy was very slow. He was still a good kid, but not up to par with the other kids his age. His father showed little interest in him.

Months came and went, and finally it was Christmas. All of the children had bought gifts for Miss Thompson, and they gathered around her desk to watch her open them. At the top of the pile, she noticed a big gift wrapped in an old brown paper bag and held together with thin strips of Scotch tape. The note written on it said, "To Miss Thompson, from Teddy Stollard." As she began to open the present, a large, gaudy, rhinestone bracelet with most of the stones missing fell to the floor. There was also a bottle of cheap perfume, the kind you buy at a five-and-dime store. All of the children began to laugh at the presents, but at least Miss Thompson had enough sense to silence them by placing the bracelet on one wrist and taking some of the perfume and dabbing it on the other. She then smelled it and held up her hand to the class, as if to say, "Gee, doesn't it smell great!" And almost as if on cue, the class oohed and aahed as if they were surprised, but the underlying tone was one of ridicule and humiliation of poor Teddy.

At the end of class that day, Teddy hung around until the last student was gone. He then walked slowly up to Miss Thompson, who was preparing to go home. He looked at her and said softly, "Gee, Miss Thompson, I'm sure glad you liked the presents. You smell just like my mother, and her bracelet sure does look pretty on you. I want to thank you and wish you a Merry Christmas."

When Teddy walked out the door, Miss Thompson dropped to her knees in that classroom and asked God for forgiveness. When the kids came to school the next day, they had a new teacher—Miss Thompson was a changed woman. She made a promise to herself to be not just a teacher but also an agent of change. She vowed to give her students something they could have long after she was gone, a piece of herself. She swore she would be there to help all of her students, particularly the slow ones, and especially Teddy Stollard.

Over the ensuing months, Teddy caught up with many of the students in the class and passed some of them by. He eventually became one of the best students in the school, surprising everyone, including himself. The years came and went, and Miss Thompson and Teddy lost track of each other. One day, as Miss Thompson was preparing to go home, she noticed there was a note in her mailbox. It read:

Dear Miss Thompson,

I have just been told I'm graduating second in my high school class and thought you should be the first to know.

Love,

Teddy Stollard

Four years later, Miss Thompson received another letter. It read:

Dear Miss Thompson,

I've just been informed I'm graduating number one in my college class. I thought you should be the first to know. It was difficult because I had to work full-time while attending the university, but I liked it.

Love,

Teddy Stollard

Another four years after that, Miss Thompson got this letter:

Dear Miss Thompson,

As of today, I am Theodore Stollard, M.D. How about that? I thought you should be the first to know. I'm getting married next week, the 27th to be exact, and would love for you to attend. You're the only family I have now. Dad died last year.

Love,

Teddy Stollard

She went to the wedding and sat where Teddy's mother would have. She had earned the right. She had given a part of herself to him that he could have long after she was gone. More importantly, she had given him something he could give to someone else.

The chain of giving, loving, and learning keeps on going. This is what life is all about. Are you just going through the motions in your life? Or are you seeking to make a difference in this world? There's no greater feeling than knowing you helped another person get to a place they never could have gotten without your influence. Money can't buy it; it is the essence of life.

As you look at the screen, seek to demonstrate behavior others will want to emulate. Become a role model. The world needs more of them! The world needs you!

The Keyboard

You have sight with your eyes, but you have insight with your mind. Anything created in this world was created because a man or woman had vision. They could see what others could not. The key is to understand that to be successful in anything, you must be able to see yourself with a much larger vision than you currently have. As long as you judge yourself by what you are and what's available to you now, you will never move from your current circumstances.

Everything starts with the power of vision in your mind's eye—insight! Imagine a tiny acorn. What do you see? Many people would answer food for squirrels. Others might say they see a mighty oak tree. Someone with insight would see commerce, industry, jobs, information, technology, and trade. It's called depth of vision. Most people focus only on what's immediately available to them. They're afraid to see themselves succeeding in a major way.

Think about your business or personal life. How do you want it to be? If you want to build a multimillion-dollar business or become an artist or a chemical engineer, don't look at where you are, look at where you can be. My grandmother always told me that it's not where you're from that counts, but where you're going.

Be Careful What You Ask for—You Might Get It!

The Peak Performers Network is a successful Minneapolis-based seminar company founded by Dan Brattland. The network conducts public seminars throughout the country in which individuals become members for a set fee and are allowed to hear a cadre of professional speakers monthly throughout the year.

I was a member of the network and went each month to hear the different speakers. It was interesting and educational. I would go not only to hear the message but also to get the feel for what the speaker's perspective was. I would go to the seminars and pretend I was watching myself instead of the speakers on the platform. As I imagined that their standing ovations were for me, I tried to capture the feeling of being up on the stage.

One day I promised myself that someday I would be on that stage at the Minneapolis Convention Center giving a seminar. I didn't know how it would happen; I just knew it would. I heard Les Brown, "the Motivator," say at a seminar one night not to worry about how something is going to happen. How it happens is none of your business. I agree!

When you start to see a larger vision of yourself, it does something to your entire thinking process. Your thoughts cause you to act with new boldness. You meet people who otherwise would never have crossed your path. You find yourself in situations where opportunities present themselves, and you ask yourself, "Where were they before?" The truth is that they were always there. You just did not see them. When I made that declaration to myself, I didn't realize my prayer would be answered much sooner than I expected.

They've Got the Right One, Baby, Uh-Huh!

I was sitting in my office at PepsiCo, Inc., minding my own business, wrapping up another day in the life of a sales manager. I was tired from the day's activities. I felt as though I were bleeding to death emotionally, one pinprick at a time, from the different problems people had unloaded on me that day. However, I did have my salvation. I had a ticket to attend a seminar that night given by Danielle Kennedy, one of the most powerful speakers in the world. It was just what I needed to get my batteries recharged. I went to seminars like these to dream, as I was trying to work my way free to speaking on a full-time basis one day, which was part of my larger vision. The seminar was to start at 7:00 P.M., just enough time for me to get home and grab a bite before heading downtown.

At 5:35, I got a call from Renée Strom, who owns the Speakers Bureau in Minneapolis. She was excited and frantic at the same time. She was talking a mile a minute, telling me I had to get to the convention center. I told her I was going down there as soon as I went home and ate, and I was excited about hearing Danielle Kennedy. She told me I didn't understand. She said Danielle Kennedy wouldn't be there; she was stranded on an airplane in Austin, Texas. Renée said Peak Performers needed a speaker and asked me if I would fill in for Kennedy. I asked how many people would be there, and she said seventeen hundred. I asked her how long they wanted me to speak, and she said three hours.

I freaked! I was so nervous I couldn't think straight. I was fumbling and mumbling. I couldn't believe this was happening. I thought, "Lord, I asked you for this blessing, but not now, okay?" I told Renée I would call her back in five minutes, after I cleared my head. She told me five minutes was all I had, because if I decided I couldn't do it, she'd need to find another speaker.

When I hung up the phone, my negative thinking took over. "Who do you think you are? You're going to go down there and make a complete fool of yourself." "You're not prepared." "You've seen good speakers who couldn't carry three hours." "You can't do it!" "Why don't you call her back and tell her you can't do it because they didn't give you enough lead time? Then you'll be off the hook."

Fortunately, there was another voice—the voice of opportunity. It told me this was my chance to shine and I'd better take it. It said, "Those folks haven't seen a real speaker yet! They don't have any idea what's about to happen tonight. I'm no stand-in! I'm the real thing."

I called Renée back three minutes and fifty-nine seconds later and told her I would do it. I left the office, pant cuffs smoking, and jumped on the freeway doing about 120 miles an hour. I went home and changed, told my wife Renée would be by to pick up some tapes to sell at the seminar, grabbed some overheads, and headed for the convention center.

My knees were knocking, and I felt like I was ready to start hyperventilating. When I saw those seventeen hundred people, it looked like the whole world. I thought, "Wow! There are going to be thirty-four hundred eyeballs on me." Talk about being under the microscope!

When they began to introduce me, I thought about my football days. Before we took the field, the team would assemble in the tunnel. We could hear the thunder of the band jamming in the stands. We would all look into the eyes of our teammates as if to say, "It's show time!"

Those were the thoughts I had as I heard the announcer from WCCO radio introduce me: "Ladies and gentlemen, after tonight you'll see why he's known throughout the country as Mr. Impact! Please help me welcome Mr. Desi Williamson." I exploded onto the stage, and for the next three hours I was in the zone.

When athletes talk about being in the zone, they mean they're performing at their best. It seems as though there is someone else at the controls switch guiding them through. It's as if some kind of divine intervention occurs. If you could capture and sell it, you would become rich overnight. That's what happened to me. The three hours went so fast, and the audience responded so well to me, I was in shock to find them standing on their feet, bestowing upon me the most precious gift a speaker can receive: a standing ovation, something that can't be manufactured. I cried as the audience stood and clapped. "They approved of me!" I thought. "I'm worthy!"

That moment marked the beginning of my professional speaking career. I learned something very valuable about myself that night: I had to believe in myself, no matter what. When your chance comes, be ready. Be careful what you wish for, because you might just get it!

Sometimes we look at other people, celebrities in particular, and find cause to ask questions like, "Lord, why didn't you give me the ability to jump like Michael Jordan, dance like Michael Jackson, or think like Albert Einstein?" Finally we come to grips with the fact we've got to play this game called life with the uniform God gives us. For the first time in my life, I felt as though I finally had the answer. I've got to become the very best Desi Williamson I possibly can. And that's good enough!

Déjà Vu Is Not an Accident

I really believe in the power of visualization. Sit back in your favorite chair sometime and relax to some of your favorite music. Close your eyes and really think about something you want to do in your life. Try to paint the picture as vividly as you can. How does it feel? What is the atmosphere like? Who are the people involved? How do the surroundings smell? The ability to be as specific as possible is very important during this little escape. The more specific you can be, the better results you will get. I did this one day as I imagined speaking to a special group of people in a very special place. It involved first-class accommodations, a limousine, the whole bit.

I was scheduled to speak at Disney World for the International Racquet, Swim and Health Association, an organization that represents health-club owners and managers all over the world. As I boarded the plane to take my seat in first class, a strange feeling came over me, as if I had done this before. I knew the flight attendant would ask me if I wanted something to drink long before she did. I looked at the magazines sitting in the rack with the feeling that *People* magazine would present itself in the pile—and it did. Déjà vu was upon me.

When I stepped off the plane in Orlando, I suspected that a man would be there with a sign that said "Mr. Desi Williamson." He was— at the expected place, standing by the gate. I asked him what kind of vehicle we were driving to the hotel, all the while thinking to myself, "I know it's a stretch limousine." Guess what? It was!

I couldn't help feeling spooky as I sat in the back of the limo, flipping all of the switches and enjoying the ride. When I got to the Swan Hotel, I was waited on hand and foot. The service was impeccable, just as I had imagined. The audience loved the speech and made me feel like part of their health-club family. I had experienced this entire trip before in my mind's eye! I thought about what a powerful tool the mind is when we take the time to use it. That's the power of vision. If you can see it, you can do it.

The Disk: Your Mental Software

We must learn to program our own minds. In the analogy to the computer, the disk represents your thoughts. Everything that's programmed into your head is just as permanent as the data programmed into the most powerful computer on earth.

Think about the Super Bowl and what a spectacle it has become. Advertisers spend as much as $1 million for a thirty-second commercial. Why? They do it in an effort to control buying decisions. These commercials all promise that your life will be better. Advertisers understand the power of learning through spaced repetition, so they play their commercials over and over. And it works. Advertisers know that when you immediately associate their tag line with their product, they've got you. We all respond like Ivan Pavlov's dogs when we hear the commercials.

Let's play a little game. Next to the tag line, write the name of the company or product it represents.

The heartbeat of America is today's _____

The King of Beers _____

Finger lickin' good _____

Don't leave home without it _____

Quality is job one _____

The real thing! _____

The choice of a new generation _____

Be all you can be! _____

How do you spell relief? _____

Winston tastes good like a _____

    The last commercial has been off the air for more than thirty years. Why do you still know it? Because you've been programmed to know it. The key thing is to be aware of the fact that each day we all receive more than two thousand messages vying for a share of our minds. Recognize that you can control your own software by programming your own mind and running it according to your own rules. You must learn to actively program your mind by the things you pay attention to and allow to become a part of your life.

I am very accommodating.
I ask no question.
I accept whatever you give me.
I do whatever I am told to do.
I do not presume to change anything you think, say, or do;
> *I file it all away in perfect order, quickly and efficiently, and*
> *then I return it exactly as you gave it to me.*
Sometimes you call me your memory.
I am a reservoir into which you toss anything your heart or
> *mind chooses to deposit there.*
I work night and day; I never rest, and nothing can impede
> *my activity.*
The thoughts you send to me are categorized and filed, and
> *my filing system never fails.*
I am truly your servant who does your bidding without
> *hesitation or criticism.*
I cooperate when you tell me you are "this" or "that" and I
> *play it back as you give it. I am most agreeable.*
Since I do not think, argue, judge, analyze, question, or make
> *decisions, I accept impressions easily. I am going to ask you*
> *to sort out what you send me, however; my files are getting*
> *a little cluttered and confused. I mean, please discard those*
> *things you do not want returned to you. What is my name?*
> *Oh, I thought you knew!*
I am your subconscious.

—Anonymous

You Produce What You Project

The first thing many people do when they come home from work is turn on the television. The average television is on eight hours a day. Now, if you sleep seven to eight hours a day, work seven to eight hours a day, and watch television the rest of the time, that's it! There isn't any more time.

Time is the most valuable resource on earth. The only thing you can do with it is use it. Television is a great invention and can be used to increase the quality of your life if you watch it selectively. There are programs with rich and vital information. If we carefully choose what we watch, the television can be a learning tool. It can also provide entertainment.

Unfortunately, many people use television as a baby-sitter, regardless of their age. When you simply "veg out" in front of it each day, you're postponing the opportunity to become more involved with your own life. What are you paying attention to? Who has you programmed on autopilot?

Once you are able to control how you focus your attention, you can control what goes into your software and ultimately what you see in the results of your life. If you have programmed your disk with the idea of limited prospects for a bright future, then this will come true.

You must zealously guard your disk. Your life depends on it! Some people bring their negative input everywhere they go. Here's my best advice about sharing your negative experiences with the world: Leave them at home. Eighty percent of the people you're telling don't care, and the other 20 percent are actually glad it's happening to you. We all have days we'd just as soon forget. There's a way to handle those days: I call them all unbelievable. From now on, when someone asks you how you're doing, tell them, "Unbelievable!" With that statement, you cover all scenarios, whether good or bad. You carry your weather with you each day, packed in a forecast called your attitude.

I am often asked by businesspeople what distinguishes top producers in any field from the middle of the pack. I say, without reservation, successful people are that way because they believe they are. They think, "Top producer, top producer, top producer!" For them, there is no other alternative. They are very conscious of how they spend their time. They read, study, and talk to people who can help them continue to be top producers. It's a way of life.

For many years, I was programmed to believe I needed eight hours of sleep a night to be effective. On nights when I didn't get eight hours, I was a basket case the next day. I spent more time worrying about the sleep I missed than I did accomplishing anything else. My disk was programmed to think "tired," so my body didn't disappoint it one bit. Now I operate with a life that's filled with vitality because my disk is programmed to think energy and vitality rather than tired and exhausted.

In your business (or any other part of life), at the end of the year, will there be top producers, those at the middle of the pack, and those at the bottom? I hope you said yes! You can pop your disk out of your head anytime you choose and program it with things that will add to the quality of your life. You can empower yourself to succeed by deciding, in advance, what kind of year you're going to have. Ask yourself some key questions about what you find yourself focusing on:

1. In what way will this experience help me become a better person?

2. Is this effect positive or negative?

3. What will be the outcome if I continue to focus my time in this way?

4. How has my lack of focus in the past hurt me?

5. How has my focus benefited me in the past?

6. How can I use the power of focus to create an even brighter future?

If you believe, as indicated by your answers to these questions, that you have a lack of ambition and are not smart enough to make your dreams come true, you will eventually play this scenario out in your behavior. You will see the results of this kind of programming when you look at the screen and replay your life. You can program the types of commercials playing in your head so they reflect a life of learning, growth, and achievement.

Another thing is to have fun. Many people don't succeed because they put too much pressure on themselves. Achievement should be fun. One of the things we should each take time to do every day is laugh. No, not just a normal laugh, but a big belly laugh! It's important to do work you love to do. This will allow you to reach your full potential and to give more to the people around you.

I encourage you to look around and count your blessings. Continually focus your attention on what's good about your life. For everything negative, there are many more positives: for every death, a birth; for every failure, yet another opportunity; for every dark night, the renewal of the following day. That's how things get done.

It's all in how you set up the software between your ears called your mind. If your life isn't what you want it to be, you must break the pattern of the kind of mental programming that's held you back. You must break free into becoming the best you you can possibly be, and not worry about meeting other people's expectations about how you should live your life.

The Value of a Smile

It costs nothing, but creates much.

It enriches those who receive, without impoverishing those who give.

It happens in a flash and the memory of it sometimes lasts forever.

None are so rich they can get along without it,

And none so poor but are richer for its benefits.

It creates happiness in a home, fosters goodwill in a business, and is the countersign of friends.

It is rest to the weary, daylight to the discouraged, sunshine to the sad, and nature's best antidote for trouble.

Yet it cannot be bought, begged, borrowed, or stolen, for it is something of no earthly good to anyone, until it is given away. And if in the hurly-burly bustle of today's world, some people you meet should be too tired to give you a smile, may we ask you to leave one of yours? For nobody needs a smile so much as those who have none left to give.

—Anonymous

CHAPTER 5
INVEST IN YOURSELF
WITHOUT HESITATION

*The apparent and tangible
are the gains evident and
within your embrace. Dreams
and plans in your heart don't
come easy. You must go meet
them face to face.*

—Saunni Dais

> *The growth of the human mind is still high adventure, in many ways the highest adventure on earth.*
>
> **—Norman Cousins**

I strongly believe that you get what you expect. In spite of all the obstacles one can use as excuses for not excelling, many people throughout history have found ways to make their dreams come true. For every person you can point out who has challenges to deal with, I can point out someone who has overcome greater challenges by getting off the ground and going for their dreams.

Work adds meaning to life, creating a sense of self-worth and accomplishment. When we believe that society owes us something, it eliminates any chance we have to gain independence through our own efforts. The concept of "something for nothing" becomes a lifelong struggle to see how much we can get for the least amount of time and effort.

This something-for-nothing mentality permeates our culture. There's no question that we live in the richest, most powerful nation in the world. Unfortunately, success often breeds complacency. Over the years, we have taken prosperity for granted, to the point where we think it should come naturally, as it did in the past. Well, the past has caught up with us! The vast and far-reaching changes in our world today have many people perplexed, frustrated, and afraid. There is hope, however, for people who are willing to use what they've got to get what they want.

As companies attempt to become more competitive in the global market, they need people who will add value to their organizations. Many misguided people think they should be rewarded for the time they've put in until now. What they don't realize is that the company can't continue to rest on past accomplishments. You must demonstrate each day the value you bring to the organization and its effect on the bottom line.

In my opinion, the operative word for the above scenario is *sacrifice*. Many people want to change their circumstances in life but are unwilling to change themselves. They remain victims, not of circumstances, but of their own way of thinking.

There's no security in employment as it was known in the past. In those days, you were paid for survival, loyalty, and time. When

America was number one in almost every economic category, life was good. Everyone was fat, dumb, and happy. We collected paychecks every other week and attempted to survive until we reached retirement. This mentality seemed to fit the times. The company took care of you as long as you kept your nose clean and didn't miss too many days of work without a serious reason. Oh, how times have changed!

The people who have the hardest time with these changes are people who want to drag this old paradigm of thinking into this new world. They believe it unreasonable for the organization to expect a justification as to what value they bring to it. They approach the new workplace kicking and screaming instead of looking in the mirror and dealing with their own deficiencies. They find blame with everyone and everything for their lack of progress. They are not willing to pay the price to upgrade their skills. The cost is not high; it just seems high to those who don't have courage or ambition enough to get off their assets.

To Survive or Succeed?

I was standing on the corner of Fourth Avenue and Pike Street in downtown Seattle, Washington, many years ago. I noticed a young man next to me begging for change. It dawned on me that he was getting exactly what he was asking for. He had extremely low expectations. He was healthy, handsome, and well-spoken. This young man did not look like a beggar.

Rather intrigued with him, I watched him in action for about fifteen minutes. Then I eased up next to him to strike up a conversation. He told me he was twenty-six, had a college education, and earned more than $25,000 a year begging. "Some of my best customers are down here," he said. This implied that many of the same people rewarded him over and over, simply for the asking.

When he walked away, I asked myself a couple of questions. What would he do to survive? Answer: He would do anything! You can't get much lower than begging, especially if you are healthy and have the capacity to produce, which he surely did. What would he do to succeed? Answer: Nothing! He would do everything to survive and nothing to succeed. My questions to you are, What are you willing to do to survive? What are you willing to do to succeed? The answers to these two questions will have a profound effect on you for the rest of your life.

You Get Paid for Value, Not Time

I don't like work, no man does, but I like what is in work, the chance to find yourself. Your own reality, for yourself, not for others, what no other man can ever know.

—Joseph Conrad

Many people working in corporations cringe when I tell them they get paid for value, not time. They feel that because they've been employed for a number of years, the company owes them a living. You must demonstrate the benefits of your employment. This goes for anyone, on any level, in any business. I tell managers that to really be effective, they must now spend no more than two days a week in their offices. They must spend the other three out on the factory floor if they're in manufacturing, out in the warehouse if they're in distribution, or on the retail floor or in the field if they're in sales.

You must spend time finding out what's going on so you can become a resource instead of a roadblock. The ones who have a problem with this are those who feel that their tenure should afford them the benefit of sitting behind a desk pushing out memos and ordering people around. Those days are gone.

Experts tell us the college graduates of today may be facing as many as twelve to fifteen different career changes during their working lives. There is, however, employment security achieved by the constant upgrading of your skills through continuing education. You cannot expect to compete in today's competitive environment unless you are willing to improve yourself through personal development.

Thanks, Mr. Rohn!

I had the opportunity to attend a seminar back in 1980 that would change things for me. The speaker, Jim Rohn, taught me several fundamental principles I'll never forget. Among the many things he said was, "You can have more than you have if you become more than you are." Another was, "Learn to work harder on yourself than you do on your job." Others included, "Don't wish things were easier, wish you were better," "Don't wish for fewer challenges, work to gain more skills," and "In order for your life to change, you've got to change." Once I was able to really peel back the onion and look at the essence of those statements, I realized I had the formula for success in my life. Mr. Rohn became my mentor, even though I didn't meet him until thirteen years later. His philosophy of life helped put me on a path to achievement.

Empowering yourself to succeed involves taking full responsibility for how your life turns out. It's taking a proactive approach to increasing your skills to a new level each and every day.

Learning Is a Lifelong Journey

When I graduated from college, I did one of the most boneheaded things a person can do: I drove by a Dumpster, took all of my books, and threw them away. I thought to myself, "Man, I'm glad all of that learning junk is over with. Now I can get on with my life!" I didn't realize that learning is a never-ending journey. The minute you stop learning, you might as well be dead.

This is important because so many people have a negative attitude about learning. It affects every aspect of their lives, especially their economic lives. Unless you know how to master computer technology, you won't be on the map in the next few years, as far as the world is concerned. You will only limit your own market viability if you refuse to work on your skills. You will earn less and suffer limited opportunities due to your skills, or lack of them. You can blame only yourself for your situation because you didn't have the courage and discipline to take action.

When you look around, you'll find that technology centered on learning has made it possible for us to learn more things in a shorter period of time than ever before. Ten years ago it was thought that the capacity for information in this world doubled every five years. Five years ago it was thought to double every three years. Today it is thought that the capacity for information in this world doubles every year. Now imagine what kind of condition you will have to be in to compete and earn a viable living if you don't make a personal-development program an ongoing part of everything you do in life. If you choose not to, no question about it, you will find yourself in serious trouble.

You are charged with the responsibility of developing your own skills on a continual basis. It's no one else's job. You must be committed enough to take the steps necessary to go back to school, to improve your reading skills, to get computer training, to increase your speaking skills. You must be willing to become a better manager, to learn new leadership skills, to become a better parent or child, to learn how to become a team player, to improve your writing skills, and to learn better health practices. Don't wait for circumstances to kick your butt! Do it yourself, ahead of time, and you will be that much further ahead in the game.

Don't Confuse Commitment and Interest

There's a huge difference between commitment and interest. When you're only interested in something, you will quit at the first sign of opposition or adversity. When you're committed, you will find a way to reach your goals no matter how long it takes or what you have to go through.

I'll never forget how my grandmother demonstrated her commitment to my education when I was in eighth grade. One evening my grandmother, my father, and I were talking at the dinner table after supper. The conversation came to where I was going to attend high school. My grandmother had told me previously I had two choices: I could attend Christian Brothers Military or St. Louis University High School. She had mentioned this to my father earlier, but nothing serious had been discussed. When she brought this up as a topic of conversation that night, my father told her I was going to attend the public school in our area like the rest of the kids in our neighborhood. My grandmother gritted her teeth and shouted, "Over my dead body!" I mean, the clock on the wall stopped. The birds flying outside halted in the air, frozen. The water I was pouring from the pitcher stopped in midstream. My father's face was also frozen. There was nothing in my grandmother's face that even looked like compromise. He was stonewalled, shut out, and the game was over. It was Nonnie 55, Daddy 0, at the end of the first quarter.

The following week my grandmother, with her wobbly aching knees, and I took three different buses out to Christian Brothers Military Academy. She waited in the hallway for three hours while

I took the entrance exam. That's what commitment is all about. The ability to do whatever it takes, no matter how long it takes.

The view from the top is the same no matter how long it takes you to get there. How committed are you to building a better life for yourself? What are you willing to do to make it happen? The rewards you receive in life will be in direct proportion to your level of personal development and skills.

Reading Is Fundamental

I was surprised to learn that one out of five American workers is illiterate. But a greater concern is aliteracy. People can read, but don't. The result for both is the same: ignorance. Many books can help people improve the quality of their lives, but people don't read them. Reading books can help you condense the amount of time it takes to do something, but you must be committed enough to explore.

Instead of going to happy hour, try going to a bookstore. You'll find it an exhilarating experience. Whatever your area of interest, there's a book on the subject. Many are written by authors who faced the same dilemma you're dealing with now. Whether it's building a fortune in real estate with no money down, creating a stronger bond with your family, or remodeling your bathroom, somebody has written a book on that subject.

Now, what do you suppose separates you from the answers you seek about how to improve your life? It's called space! The only thing holding you back is your own ability to put your feet in motion. For this reason, I believe it is essential to spend a portion of each day engaged in a personal-development program. Reading one hour a day will change your life. It will take your mind on journeys you otherwise would never experience. Reading will allow you to explore dimensions of your own consciousness and help you become a more powerful person.

Zig Ziglar has long been one of my favorite people. His contributions in the field of self-development speak for themselves. I had the opportunity to meet him at one of his seminars many years ago. I was impressed that well into his seventies, he spends three hours each day working to increase his skills through personal development. Now that's commitment! Are you willing to invest the time it takes to get better? Are you willing to take control of your life now? I encourage you to start now, right where you are.

Become a Twenty-first-Century Person

I am blessed to work with senior managers for some of the most powerful corporations in the world. I often ask human-resource managers what they feel are the key skills needed to succeed in today's competitive environment. Some of the answers follow.

Communication Skills: The ability to express yourself one-on-one or in large or small groups is a skill that will help separate you from the pack.

I've met people who have strong educational backgrounds but lack the interpersonal skills necessary to succeed. Many are unaware that the lack of these vital skills is a shortcoming for them until someone is candid enough to point it out. They can bounce around for years in frustration, going from interview to interview, and often taking jobs that are far less challenging than their level of skill would warrant.

You must continue to improve your oral and written communication skills. The higher you go in business, the stronger these skills need to be, for at each progressively higher level, there are people who are more adept at these skills. This separates people who enjoy greater responsibility, faster advancement, and higher incomes from people with the same background but weaker communication skills.

Starting tomorrow, craft for yourself a game plan that includes books, tapes, and classes on how to improve your communication skills. There are many associations that will help you, such as Toastmasters and the National Speakers Association, which happen to have chapters in each state.

Computer Skills: You must become skilled in computer technology in order to succeed in the future.

I was initially horrified at the prospect of having to learn about computers. I bought a computer and left it in the box for weeks before summoning the courage to set it up. Then I decided that if I was going to become the kind of businessman I wanted to be, getting on board the technology train was critical. I enrolled in a series of computer classes and immediately began to feel more comfortable. With each class, my skill level increased, and now I find myself helpless without my computer.

It's interesting what happens when we move past our fears and take the plunge. Whether you are working for a large corporation or engaged in your own small business, you need to be computer literate. Why not get started now? Go for it!

Become a Team Player: People who can successfully interact with others remain among the most attractive candidates for any organization.

Interaction calls on many skills, such as communication, listening, and the ability to subordinate personal interests for the good of the team. I've seen many instances where lack of teamwork destroyed the business. I once worked in an environment where the inability of management and the union to work together almost ruined the company. It wasn't until the very existence of the organization was put at risk that they realized there soon wouldn't be anything to argue about. They moved from looking for who was right to trying to find out what was best. When you have learned to collaborate with other people successfully, you have developed a universal skill and will be more marketable.

Become Adaptable to Change: In my travels, I often hear people say, "Man, I sure will be glad when this change stuff is over and things get back to normal." I immediately tell them, knocking on my forehead with my fist, "Hello, this is normal!" You should understand that because the world is in a constant state of change, you must be open-minded enough to continue trying new things.

There's No Way Around Education

I believe there are two kinds of education: formal education and street knowledge. One without the other is automatically weak; for balance, you need both. We've all heard about or met an educated fool, a person who is well versed technically speaking but lacks the common sense to walk around the block without getting lost. There's also the street urchin, the person who is streetwise but doesn't know how to communicate. The only way to become proficient in both areas is to seek knowledge in each one.

If you're lacking in formal education, you must figure out what you're interested in, and then you must find out who has the knowledge in that area. After that, you must devote time, effort, and energy to pursuing this information. This often involves starting at the bottom level of an organization and learning the business from the ground up. I meet many young people who are far too impatient. They want to be CEO of the corporation right now! You must recognize that until you learn something, you don't know it. Unfortunately, no business, large or small, can afford to roll the dice of its future based on what you think you know.

I spend quite a bit of time talking with college athletes. It's very hard to get them to understand that most of them will not play pro sports. In all of the major sports, there are fewer than three thousand athletes who play professionally. The University of Minnesota has a counseling day each year when several former pro football players and I come in to talk with student athletes about the value of education. It's amazing to see the look in the students' eyes when former players tell them they have a better chance of hitting the lottery than they do of playing professional sports. They don't believe it. Each one thinks he is going to be the one who makes it big. Many don't take their education seriously and end up in serious trouble.

I'm always the last to speak that day, I tell them that I was once sitting right where they are, thinking the same thing: "I'm going to the pros!" I say to them, "Among all of the speakers you see here today, I'm the only one who didn't play pro ball." I tell them that the pros is exactly where most of them are not going. This immediately gets their heads up. They are no longer slumped over in their chairs, looking cool. I say, "Oh, I see I have your attention now."

I play out a scenario for them by assuming that one of them does get drafted and ends up with a pro team. My question then becomes, "Why is it so many professional athletes end up broke?" They look at me deadpan. How can a person sign a multimillion-dollar contract and within a few years have nothing? It's because their income took a leap beyond their mentality to deal with it. Because they didn't mature to the level necessary to keep pace with the money, it came back to meet their level of education. If they end up broke, what does that tell you about their level of personal development and education? It is obviously not up to par.

Now let's analyze something further. Who ends up with all of their money? The people with education, that's who. The agents, lawyers, and businesspeople all have educations and are poised to pounce on people less versed in the nuances of business than they are. There is no getting around education. When athletes retire, most often, they are in their early thirties. How are they going to make a living for their more than forty years of life left?

If you don't know something, then you'd better know someone who does. I call it the power of OPs. There's other people's money, other people's time, other people's energy, other people's knowledge—the list goes on. The key is to use, not misuse, these resources to increase your odds of winning. Build yourself a team of people who are highly skilled in the areas where you may be lacking. They, in turn, can use the skills you bring, creating a win-win proposition for all.

The Minute You Think You've Arrived, Look Out!

If you're egotistical enough to believe you have all of the skills you need, you are sure to be replaced in a short time. Your own ignorance will be the reason. Long-term success comes to people who continually seek ways to get better. When you approach the future with this attitude, you have the formula for changing your life. Success is never a place where you can stay without continual learning; technology is changing too fast. Just imagine the number of inventions that are on the drawing board we haven't even heard of yet. It can be daunting!

Avoid Information Overload

Do you ever feel frustrated when zeroing in on what to learn? I do. I've had more than my share of headaches trying to determine where to start. The key for me has been to decide on a definite course of action. When I prioritize according to needs, I focus on the things that will give me the greatest return for the time invested.

Take the time to craft a plan of action for yourself by deciding what things are most important for you to learn first. List why it's important for you to learn these things and what you expect to gain from them over the short and long term. This will keep you from feeling overwhelmed with all of the information coming to you. It's similar to a smorgasbord. On it, you find a tremendous amount of choices, but there's no way you can eat them all. You choose some things and bypass others. This will give you a greater feeling of control as you face the information age.

Don't Confuse Cost and Worth

I believe your life will change when you decide to invest in yourself without hesitation. I have a library in my house that has taken me years to build. Books line the shelves, along with audio and video training programs. People often ask to borrow my books or tapes. I very kindly give them the names of the authors and the prices and tell them where I purchased the material. Many are insulted.

Some complain about the price. I tell them that instead of asking what something costs, they should be more concerned about what it's worth. They are asking the wrong question! I ask them if they are truly committed to learning or simply interested. If they are merely interested, they probably wouldn't read or listen to the information if I gave it to them anyway. If they are truly committed to learning, they will make the investment necessary. Here's another thing: Whenever I loaned my material to people, I never got the stuff back. I had to replace many hundreds of dollars' worth of materials before I learned this valuable lesson.

Many people hold themselves back because they are too cheap with themselves. They aren't willing to invest the time and financial resources to get ahead. They spend money on things that will provide temporary satisfaction and offer nothing that will help them build a better future.

You must be willing to bet on you. If you don't, why should anyone else? This saying has never been more true: "If you take the coins from your purse and fill your mind, your mind will eventually fill your purse with coins." I've seen the results of this philosophy in my life.

You must make the distinction between what something costs and what it's worth. When you do, you take a huge step toward understanding that your own personal growth and development is the key to your future. There is employment security; you achieve employment security by working on your core competencies.

Please don't shortchange yourself! The market will reward you. The information that can help you change your life is not in short supply. If you could afford to purchase this book, then you are already familiar with the process. Now just keep doing it over and over and over again, for the rest of your life.

CHAPTER 6
DEALING WITH THE CHALLENGE OF CHANGE

Challenge is a necessary prerequisite for continued growth. Its first cousin, change, recycles probabilities, potential and hope.

—**Saunni Dais**

> *God, give us grace to accept with serenity the things that cannot be changed, courage to change the things which should be changed, and the wisdom to distinguish the one from the other.*
>
> **—Reinold Niebuhr**

How many of us stick with old ways of doing things or old behaviors long after they've proven outdated and ineffective? Sometimes it seems as though we must wait until our pant cuffs are on fire before we get off our duffs and do something. Don't wait until you're on fire or in trouble to change, because you could wait too long!

My oldest brother defied everything my father told him to do. My father would take him to school and occasionally even walk him to the classroom. As soon as the car sped off, my brother would skip out of school and go right back to the pool hall.

This went on for years. One night he didn't come home. My father became worried. At 3:00 A.M. the phone rang. It was the police department, explaining that my brother had been shot in the neck. My brother lived in a wheelchair for seven years before his body deteriorated; he died at the age of twenty-four. The day before his death he was staring out the window. I eased up and asked him what he was thinking. He said he was looking back over the course of his life and thinking he really wanted to change. He said he had always told himself he would, but unfortunately he didn't and was now paying the price. He told me, "Desi, it's not enough to just change. Man, you've got to change in time!" I get chills every time I think about that day.

My youngest brother, André, had the same attitude as my oldest brother. He felt he could beat the system. Although a straight-A student, he challenged authority at every turn and loved to get into mischief. As a teenager he went from one reform school to another. He was intellectually brilliant, but he always used his smarts for deviousness. Finally, he took to robbing banks and successfully pulled off several robberies. Simply using a note that said, "Put the money in the bag or I'll blow your head off!" he was able to rob more than a dozen banks. He got away each time.

His day of reckoning came when he went to a dealership to purchase a car. When he put down $20,000 in cash without any evidence of employment, the dealer became suspicious, to say the least. As André exited his apartment one morning, he was stunned to find that he was surrounded by police officers and state troopers with their guns loaded, cocked, and aimed at him.

He spent the last twelve years in prison. As I mentioned in chapter 2, he called me from the penitentiary after a few years and told me he had finally figured out why he was there. "Desi, it took me a long time to come to grips with the fact that I'm the reason I'm in prison," he said. I began to cry. He said another important thing then, too: He said he had wished for many things over the years, but most of all, he'd wished he would have changed in time.

Of the many abusive relationships my mother had, one had deadly consequences. She was married to a rough-and-tumble biker named Jerry. He would beat her up and then go out on a drinking or drug binge. Then he would come back and do it again. When I would go to visit her, he would act like the sweetest guy in the world, only to return to beating my mother when I left. She kept this from me because she didn't want me to worry or get involved. I was a child, and she felt she could handle the situation.

This went on for years. One day he came home and beat her so badly she had to go to the hospital. But before he could leave this time, she took a .38-caliber revolver and emptied it into his body, killing him. Later she told me she had always thought about putting him out of her house but somehow always found reasons not to. She told me that even if you kill in self-defense, you still suffer unimaginable feelings of guilt and regret that come from the taking of a life. Leaving this relationship in time could have prevented this terrible tragedy.

The tragedy of my brothers' lives taught me that it's not enough to change; you've got to change in time. In business, you've got to change before opportunity is lost. Many people are waiting for conditions to determine what they are going to do. You must realize that the only time things are going to change in your life is when you change.

Don't wait until your situation is terminal or you'll live with regret, and when you try to change things, it may be too late!

Why Is Change So Hard?

Change is very difficult, but if you continue to do the things you've been doing, you'll continue to get the same results. Try crossing your arms in the traditional fashion, with your left arm folded over your right one. Now switch positions, with your right arm now placed over your left. Does it feel a bit awkward? Of course it does. It always will.

Every time you seek to make a change in your life, it will feel uneasy at first. You must be willing to work through it. This uneasiness is one of the reasons so many people live lives filled with failure and regret. They are not willing to be uncomfortable long enough to grow. You must be willing to operate with a certain degree of uncertainty if you want to become more than you currently are. Change is a process, and it requires patience. Often, you will not see results immediately, but you must stay the course nevertheless. Resilience plays a huge role in implementing any lasting changes in your life. You cannot let temporary setbacks deter you from the changes.

Stuck on Stupid

There was a guy who used to walk around campus at the University of Minnesota. We all called him "Walking Phil." He was quite a contradiction. He looked like a bum, always wearing tattered clothing, with an old fishing hat perched on top of his head. He walked with a real strut and always carried a copy of the *Wall Street Journal*. He could always be found walking through an area of campus called Dinky Town, which had restaurants and bars where students hung out. He loved to stop students and, in particular, athletes.

I always seemed to be unfortunate enough to catch his eye whenever I was on my way to practice or to and from class. He would grill me as to whether or not I was attending class on a regular basis and taking care of business. He smelled so bad I would often have to take a step back. Walking Phil was extremely articulate and spoke with as much confidence as he exuded when he walked. He even gave me a stock tip one day that I later checked out with a broker; it was one of the fastest-growing companies in the country.

I could never quite figure Walking Phil out. He was a paradox. How could such a smart man be in such dire circumstances? Walking Phil has been walking around campus for better than thirty years now. I still see him from time to time when I'm around the university.

I did some investigating and found that Walking Phil has a master's degree and a Ph.D. from the University of Minnesota. After graduating he had fallen madly in love with a woman who eventually left him for someone else. He snapped and has never been the same.

This one incident in life caused Walking Phil to get stuck. He lacked resiliency. The ability to bounce back is what separates winners from losers. Walking Phil is stuck on stupid, and it's ridiculous for him to give up on his entire life because of a soured relationship. I'm sure that woman has gotten on with her life and probably doesn't spend much time thinking about him. As smart as this man is, he remains ignorant in terms of the wisdom necessary to move on.

The Philosophy of *Next!*

Let's say you're in a doctor's office, waiting, and a patient goes in before you. Let's say the patient dies. Does the doctor come out and say, "Well, that last patient died, so we're closing." I don't think so! The doctor will come out of his office into the waiting room. He will look to the left and then to the right and say one word: "Next!" Let's say another patient comes in and dies. They send him down the chute into a big box that awaits him in the alley. Does the doctor's office close? No! The doctor comes out of his office into the waiting room. He looks to the right and then looks to the left and says, "Next!" It's always *Next!*

In the past, when I gave a seminar, I would be disappointed if everyone didn't leave excited. I would often blame myself for the one or two people who would give me negative feedback on my evaluations. I would ask myself, "What seminar were they attending?" After a while I came to the conclusion that some people get it and some don't. Some will use the material and some won't. I'm not responsible for that; they are.

My philosophy of life has changed over the years to *Next!* It doesn't matter if they say, "Desi, we love you and we're gonna get in there with you and burn it up in five seconds!" I say, "Great—next!" If they say, "We think you stink and are the worst speaker we've ever heard," I say, "Great—next!"

Next is all you have. You cannot spend years dwelling on a situation that has long since past. Walking Phil could probably have been a successful lawyer, doctor, or politician. When that woman left him, after getting the crying out of his system, he should have stood up, dusted himself off, and yelled at the top of his voice, "Next!" I suggest you do the same thing.

The Increasing Impact of Change

There are important reasons for the increasing impact of change. There's no guarantee that what is working for you now will work even as long as tomorrow. New ways of doing things and new products, services, and philosophies make it necessary for you to adapt.

When you feel as if change is coming at you at a faster rate than you can handle, the natural tendency is to become overwhelmed. We all come into this world with an imaginary bucket of water. Have you ever gotten to the point where your bucket was full? If someone tried to dump more in it but it was overflowing, you exploded by saying, "Get your own bucket, Jack, because mine is full!"

We also come into this world with a certain number of assimilation credits. These credits represent the amount of tolerance each of us has for change. We all deal with it in different ways, but each time you are faced with change, you use a certain number of assimilation credits to make the transition. These credits are the water pouring into your bucket.

I have identified three different kinds of change: macro, organizational, and micro. Macro change involves interest rates, tax rates, who's president, and the price of a paper clip. It involves things that are outside of your ability to control but that you can still influence—with your vote, for example.

Organizational change occurs when your company asks you to switch jobs to give the organization more bench strength, enabling you to become a more valued employee by learning different skills. If you own your own business, it involves making changes because of market demands. For example, when the tax laws changed in the mid-eighties, it forced wholesale changes in the real estate industry. The macro change of tax reform caused organizational change within every business affected by it.

Micro change is when something affects you personally. Anyone who has ever had their house broken into, been divorced, had major medical problems arise, or had a close relative of theirs die has been faced with a micro change in their life. This is the level of change that requires the largest number of assimilation credits for adaptation. Once your bucket is full of life's changes, it overflows, just like water in a bucket when the faucet is left running. It is at this point that you feel stress. A remedy is needed.

If you have a glass and it is filled to the rim with water, can you get the glass to hold any more water? The answer is yes—if you pour some of the contents of the glass out first. Life is the same way. You must be willing to give up something in order to get something. Holding on to old beliefs or ways of doing things because they are comfortable is an ironclad guarantee that your life will not change in any significant way.

Change does not always have to come by means of things that are done to you. I call this the "victims of circumstance" syndrome. You can implement changes in your life anytime you decide to, simply by making key decisions. I know people involved in jobs and relationships they know are not in their best interest, but they stay, stay, and stay—until circumstances push them out on a limb. Meanwhile, they have lost the most precious commodity: time. Make the changes before they make you!

Understanding How Change Feels

When undergoing change, the first thing you will think about is what you are giving up—which, in some cases, ain't much! You may feel alone. You may feel as if the whole world is coming down on you and you can only handle so much change. Give yourself a break, because people are at different readiness levels for change.

You may have to start slowly, but, please, get started! You may worry that you don't have enough resources, which is often a concern when people start their own businesses. Get started with what you have, right now. Remember also to hold yourself to certain standards of behavior, because if you don't, you will revert back to your old habits, and nothing will happen. You must work through the initial pain you may have to endure. Believe me, it will pale in comparison next to the pain of regret you will experience as you look back over the course of your life and know you didn't do what you should have.

Life is no dress rehearsal. You only go around once. When it comes to change, it's "no pain, no gain." Let me say that the temporary discomfort is well worth it. You will become a different person because you will know in your heart you've got what it takes to make things happen in your life.

Change Yourself First

Change requires you to adjust your attitude. Don't think about the things you may be losing because those things may be the ones that are holding you back. Don't think, "There's no way I can do this." Think to yourself, "Sure, this is tough, but so am I! I can and will handle this!" Make positive affirmations to yourself and say them both aloud and silently each day. Use the action guide in the back of this book. It will help you tremendously.

You must be willing to let go of your past. When people are trying to hold on to the past, they go through periods of denial by saying, "This doesn't mean anything. I'll just hang out and things will get back to normal." When they are asked to make changes on their jobs, they immediately say, "How can they do this to me?" "I hate doing things this way," or "Poor little me." When this doesn't work, they begin bargaining with change. They say, "Okay, I'll do this part the way that change dictates, but I'm keeping all other parts the same." Still, some people act as if to say, "I don't care what they say, I'm not changing no matter what!"

Here's what you need to understand right now. Change doesn't care how you feel. It is not going to ask for your permission. Change just is. When it comes, it waits for no one. The question is, Are you ready? When you get those subtle signs that you need to make a change in your life, do you ignore them or do you act?

Moving from Neutral to Overdrive

What a wonderful life I've had! I only wish I'd realized it sooner.

—Colette

Some people go through their lives in neutral. They act as if they believe that if they postpone making a decision, the situation will go away. It never does. You decide what it will take to move from neutral into drive and then overdrive. Don't worry about having to do everything right at the beginning. Make a commitment to keep trying.

You never know what you are capable of unless you try. When you take the first step toward change, you will move to a new beginning and start a new chapter in the story of your life.

A Plan for Life Change

1. Weigh the pros and cons of the change. If the pros outweigh the cons, it's time to try something new. Do it now. Don't wait another day to make the necessary changes.

2. Break the desired change into small parts. Write a specific statement of affirmation for each change and a definite deadline for its accomplishment.

3. Enter into a written contract with a close friend or coworker who can serve as a compassionate observer or coach. Make sure, though, that it is someone who will hold you to your promise as stated.

4. Start with the easiest part of the change. Give yourself a fighting chance.

5. Write a statement of positive self-talk. Think about all the reasons why this will work and how you will benefit from making the changes. Make this your focus from now on.

6. Work on one change at a time. Complete one part of the change process before moving on to something else.

7. Be patient. To change a behavior, you must practice it for at least thirty days consecutively.

8. Recognize that change will be awkward at first, but that once you get the hang of it, things will seem no different than before, except you will be much better off.

9. Celebrate your success, no matter how small.

Key Questions

1. What do you want to change about your life?

2. How do you want to go about making the changes?

3. When do you want to make the changes?

4. Are you absolutely committed to changing your life for the better?

Change Tips

Learn to change yourself first. Don't worry about trying to change someone else. Remember: Change is good, change is necessary, change is imminent, and change takes time, but . . . *don't take too long!*

CHAPTER 7
UNLEASH YOUR GOAL POWER

Goal Tending

*Belief will manifest your
presence if you can fashion
the magic of focus.*

*Will exerted can forge
the mystery, oft times
yielding honorable notice.*

*Synergy stands ready to aid your
grand and truly heartfelt dreams.*

*Watch out, my friend,
for the "Doubt Most Monster"
that cannibalizes esteem!*

—**Saunni Dais**

*Nothing contributes so much to tranquilize the mind as a
steady purpose, a point on which the soul may fix its
intellectual eye.*

—**Mary Wollstonecraft Shelley**

When I was growing up in St. Louis, on any summer night you could go downtown near the St. Louis County Jail and hear the inmates yelling and screaming out of their cell windows. I would often wonder how they ended up that way. It always scared me to think that with a few wrong moves and bad decisions on my part, I could end up in the same place, yelling out of a jailhouse window and wondering how in the world I got there in the first place.

I will never forget when I got caught stealing from a small neighborhood grocery store. We had moved into a rather tough neighborhood, and I'd started to hang out with some tough kids. To be accepted, I had to prove myself every day. If challenged, I had to deal with it. My nerve, courage, and will were tested. If I was deemed to be weak, I was finished; people would prey on me each day, taking my money, clothes, and anything of mine that they perceived had value. Many of these kids came from large families, and if I happened to get into a fight with one of them, I would literally be fighting for weeks as they all stood in line for a shot at me.

That's how I ended up in that store with a Lucky Cake in my coat pocket. Other kids had been stealing from this store and had not been caught. If I wanted to be initiated into the gang, I'd have to pass this test. If I didn't do it, I was risking constant beatings and harassment from gang members.

The game went like this: We would all go into the store and some kids would pretend to be looking at items to purchase while I stole Lucky Cakes from the bakery section. I didn't realize that the couple who owned the store were watching me through one of the strategically placed mirrors. As I stepped to the counter to purchase the penny candy as my ruse, the woman said to me, "Hey, what do we have here?" Her husband, a huge man, grabbed me and threw me into the meat locker with the cold cuts, still uncut and hanging from the ceiling. He told me he was going to call the police and have me picked up. I began yelling and screaming, "Mister, please let me out! I'm sorry! I promise I will never come back into your store again! I didn't mean to steal from you!"

I didn't fear the police as much as the beating my mother would have given me had she found out about it. I knew she would skin me alive! All I could see was that ironing cord whipping across my backside.

Fortunately, after listening to me scream for the better part of twenty minutes, the owner felt sorry for me and let me go. Before he did, he told me that if I didn't change my ways, I would end up in prison one day. He also said he could tell I wasn't a hard kid, and I should stop hanging out with the gang. He said he knew some of them had stolen things from his store, but he hadn't caught them yet. I thought, "Why me?" At the age of ten, I'd gotten a valuable lesson that helped to detour me from further stealing, but not quite yet.

Heroes Can Help

After moving to a better neighborhood in the suburbs, we seemed to have a new lease on life. I went to an integrated school for the first time in my life. My brother and I were able to make friends quickly. We developed a relationship with two boys about our ages who lived across the street, Ronnie and Adrian. I envied them because they were from a wholesome family with very strict parents who really made them toe the line but were also kind. Their father was a huge man of few words. You could tell he was no one to fool with. The last thing in the world the two boys wanted was to experience the wrath of their father.

There was a vending company just two blocks from our houses, and my brother and I talked Ronnie and Adrian into robbing one of the trucks while the place was closed. One night after closing, the four of us took bricks, knocked out the windows of one of the trucks, and hit the jackpot.

We had more candy, gum, and soda pop than most stores. We made off with the goods in a shopping cart and hid them in an abandoned building. We thought we had gotten away with something, but we hadn't. Our consciences would not allow us to sleep at night. The next day, we saw the Marvel comic book cartoons on television for the first time. We decided we would each adopt one of the characters—Thor,

Captain America, Spiderman, and the Submariner—and become them, doing what was right from that day forward. We took the stolen goods back to the owner and told him what had happened and how sorry we were. We also pleaded with him not to tell our parents. He promised he wouldn't. He told us that since we had the courage to come forth, we had learned a valuable lesson about life, and that was more valuable than any subsequent discipline. Thank goodness! Had my mother found out about this, she might still be whipping me to this day.

Many young people end up in miserable circumstances because they have not learned how to set goals. Many people are dead but haven't left us yet—they're the walking dead. They live their lives with no clear sense of direction or purpose. They have no goals. Once I committed myself to the process of goal setting, my life changed immensely, and it has never been the same since. I promise that if you will allow yourself to become engulfed in the process of planning your life, it will reward you accordingly. The key is to first decide what you want and then put a plan of action into place.

It's a sad fact that most people spend more time planning a vacation than they do setting goals. If you don't have goals, you will surely drift through life and, more often than not, you will not be happy with the outcome. You must decide for yourself what you want out of life and commit it to pencil and paper just as you would write a contract.

The Coach Who Would Be King

I really admire Lou Holtz, who coached at the University of Notre Dame. He had to overcome great odds. Growing up in East Liverpool, Ohio, he was a scrawny little kid with a lisp. One of his teachers told him he didn't have brain power enough to graduate from Kent State University.

He was coaching at the University of William and Mary when the entire coaching staff was fired. His wife was pregnant with their third child. He said later that he had never been so depressed and despondent in his entire life. Coach Holtz also said he made a commitment to do something that would change the course of his life. He sat down with a pen and paper and wrote down more than one hundred things he wanted to do with his life. He set goals to appear on the *Tonight Show*, land on an aircraft carrier, and play some of the world's famous golf courses, all of which he eventually did. One of his goals was to be head football coach at the University of Notre Dame. After coaching at the University of Minnesota and taking a team that had finished a dismal 1–10 two years before to a bowl game, he achieved his goal of coaching at Notre Dame.

Lou Holtz set goals and made the commitment to see them through. You can do the same thing. You must be disciplined and care about your life enough to think about it and write out a detailed game plan. This is your blueprint for the future.

Part of the price for success is goal setting. Any business starts out each year with a business or annual operating plan. No business is more serious than that of living your life. If you don't take the time to set goals, be prepared to accept whatever comes your way. After reading this chapter and doing the exercises in the action guide at the end of the book, you will be ready to realize your dreams and reach for the stars.

Find Some Mentors

We can all make excuses for not setting goals in life for fear they won't come true. I've heard people ask, "Why even try to do this or that? No other person has ever done that." I felt that way about professional speaking. I had a mental block because I didn't see any examples of successful black speakers in the industry. I'm not talking about athletes who do the lecture circuit, for few of them can be categorized as professional speakers. Many are simply athletes who speak. I wanted to see someone who had come from a similar or worse background than mine yet was making it, and I saw no one.

I was working for PepsiCo, Inc. I was doing well in my job, but I had always had a burning desire to become a professional speaker. I picked up the Yellow Pages one day and looked under "Training." I found Professional Sales Trainers, which taught the Tom Hopkins training curriculum. I called the owner and asked if they were hiring trainers. He told me they weren't; he hadn't found anyone he trusted enough to leave one of his classes with, but he was interested in potential salespeople.

I went on to talk with him, not about becoming a salesperson but about becoming a speaker. I asked him if he was willing to let me pay to take his class. Afterward, I asked him to give me just one opportunity to stand before the class and give a presentation, and if he didn't like what he heard, we would forget all about the prospects of my doing any training for him.

He took me up on my offer, and I taught the night training class for him for three years. He and I made some big plans. We began to change the curriculum of the program, and we moved from a video facilitation format to teaching every aspect of the program ourselves. I got better and better at it. We spent time together every Saturday creating and designing new material.

I thought we were going to build a business together, and I was crushed when I was told he no longer needed me. I was convinced I needed him. I had become dependent. I believed that he could get into doors I couldn't because he was white. I figured I could sneak in the back door behind him and get noticed. I was crushed because I felt that this was my one chance. That I saw no other black speakers doing what I wanted to do gave me a convenient and temporary excuse for giving up on my dream.

At that time, I seemed to find solace in what I believed were legitimate reasons for not moving another step forward. I later learned something very valuable: There's always somebody out there! I needed a sign. I asked for one, and it was provided. Please, read on.

The Turning Point

The turning point for me came on a restless Sunday afternoon in 1984. I was flipping through cable channels when I ran across Les Brown on BET (Black Entertainment Television). He was dynamic, exciting, and doing what I wanted to do. He talked about how you had to enlarge your vision of yourself. He said you had to believe in yourself.

Les was from a negative background similar to mine, and had suffered with misery and disappointments. I immediately got off the couch and began to take notes. Les talked about how you've got to be *hungry*.

When I saw him that day, it changed my life. I thought to myself, "Here's a black man who's doing what I've been thinking about. If he can do it, so can I!" When I saw Les Brown, I no longer had an excuse.

Whatever you want to do in life, someone else has done it before. I made it a goal to meet Les Brown. I didn't know when or how it would happen. He has often said setting the goal is the major thing; how it gets reached is none of your business! I believe that goal setters are pace setters.

I got a call one day from Renée Strom of the Speakers Bureau in Minneapolis. She told me Les Brown had asked about me and wanted to talk to me. She gave me the phone number of his hotel in New York. I called him immediately. He said he had heard good things about the work I was doing and wanted to congratulate me. He was putting together a cadre of speakers to travel the country and speak to different organizations. He asked me to send him my material. My goal setting had worked. Just a few years earlier I had written that one day I would meet this man; I didn't know when, but I knew it would happen.

I have had many other mentors even though I've never met most of them personally. When I first decided I wanted to start a real estate business, I sought out two books. They were *Nothing Down* and *Creating Wealth*, by Robert Allen. I used his philosophy to get where I wanted to go at a much faster rate. Since reading his books I have amassed a substantial real estate portfolio.

You can find and use mentors the same way. These people can help you increase the quality of your life and accelerate your progress. Mentors help you gain confidence if you are disciplined enough to read and listen to their work, and then take appropriate action on the ideas that stimulate you most. In their stories, you will find the courage to write your own script and build your life to order. You will find that some of them overcame tremendous obstacles to achieve their dreams. Some I've used over the years include Dr. Norman Vincent Peale, Mary Kay Ash, Mary Parker Follet, Napoleon Hill, Dr. Martin Luther King Jr., Dr. Robert Schuller, Jim Rohn, Muhammad Ali, Tony Robbins, Les Brown, John Johnson, Donald Trump, Russell Conwell, George Clason, and Og Mandino. They all have one thing in common: They all had goals that drove them to take action and get the results they wanted from their lives.

When you set goals, your mind gains focus and your body performs the activities necessary to help you achieve. You must learn to trust this process. In my years of formal education, no one ever taught me to set goals. I didn't learn to until I was twenty-four years old, and my life has never been the same. I travel to speak to Fortune 500 companies, and I'm the author of four audiotape programs, a videotape series, and this book. I earn as much money in one month as I previously earned in a year. I can only tell you that all of this comes from setting goals.

Think of all the things you take for granted. For most of us, learning to drive a car was, at one time, a goal. Once we learned to do it, we moved on to something else because we took for granted that this goal had been accomplished. The key thing here is to understand the process by which you achieve something. Once you have been successful doing something, you have proven to yourself that you can be successful. The main objective is to move from simple successes to higher and higher levels.

On New Year's Eve, I sat down at 6:00 A.M. to craft my goals for the year. I've done this for twenty years now. I can't imagine my life without them. Without written goals, I would never have gotten to the point of writing this book—also once a written goal now accomplished.

Where Do You Start?

Even if you're on the right track, you'll get run over if you just sit there.

—Will Rogers

Start wherever you are right now. The time will never be more right! Don't let another day go by without taking the time to assess your situation and make definite plans to change your life into what you want it to be. No matter how dire your circumstances may seem, you have the ability to plan your way out of them. It's all a matter of perspective.

During the stock market crash of 1929, many people lost all of their money. People committed suicide in record numbers. Others resorted to begging in the streets. But at the same time, some people became millionaires. Many of the people who succeeded probably had some idea of what they wanted to do and how they wanted to go about achieving it.

Today we are faced each day with the national debt, corporate layoffs, and softness in the economy, all of which cause people to live with fear and apprehension. Believe me, you cannot afford to take chances by guessing what the future holds for you. You must know where you want to go, how you plan to get there, and when you expect to arrive.

Stop Procrastinating, Now!

When you get right down to the root of the meaning of the word "succeed," you find it simply means to follow through.

—F. W. Nichol

Whatever it is you want to do with your life, you've got to start taking action immediately. When I was eighteen years old and forty seemed like it was far in the future, I used to say, "Man, that's old!" I was working out with some young guys once at a health club when one of them asked me how old I was. When I told him forty, he said, "Man, that's old!" I thought to myself, "Wait a minute—that's my line! I'm the one who used to say that to older guys. Now I'm one of them." We have got to make sure we don't get left behind—time waits for no one.

Don't let spring, summer, winter, or fall keep you from the task of setting goals. Goal setting can be more demanding than physical labor; this thinking forces you to deal with the depths of your being. It requires you to answer tough questions about yourself, and sometimes you will find you don't have answers to important issues in your life. That's okay. Goal setting will help lead you to answers in many cases. Many times a goal in one area of your life will lead you to answers in another, but you can never find them if you aren't willing to struggle. Whether in family, career, health, financial, spiritual, social, or recreational areas, you must develop the courage to design your life.

You must learn to master the ability to focus. You cannot afford to let the telephone, dust in the corners of your office, a sunny day, or anything else get you off track. You have to learn to say *no!* You will have interruptions, and they will always seem to happen during the time you have set aside for goal setting. This used to happen to me constantly, and it provided me with a convenient excuse to put goal setting off again. It often left me out of time and energy to do the necessary things to keep my own house in order.

Now if someone comes by unannounced or calls for social talk in the middle of something important, such as planning, I simply tell them I'm busy. If they push, I tell them to let me call them back or stop by at a more convenient time for the both of us—I've got to keep moving. Sometimes we don't do this; we feel we will alienate a friend or an acquaintance. Nothing could be further from the truth. If a person is in your corner, they'll understand and appreciate the fact that you're trying to increase the quality of your life. If they can't, maybe you need to reevaluate whether or not this person is really a friend.

Many people spend years putting things off for what they perceive to be a little bit better time. First, they don't have the ability to distinguish between what's urgent and what's important. The urgent is often the easier of the two to attend to but often provides the least reward in terms of real productivity. Second, they haven't become disciplined enough to make a real commitment to setting goals and will continue to get the same or worse results because they have not made any significant changes. Finally, many people suffer from the mañana syndrome, saying, "I'll get around to that tomorrow." Unfortunately, tomorrow never comes. This deadly disease is one of the main reasons for failure. You have to just do it!

Goal Setting Can
Set You Free Financially

I'll never forget one very important goal-setting moment. I was sitting in a hotel in Rapid City, South Dakota, one evening in 1985, bored out of my mind. I decided that to become more productive, I would spend the evening focusing entirely on some goal setting. I was earning about $40,000 a year at the time. I set a goal to pay myself a certain amount of money each time I received a paycheck, which was then every two weeks. I wrote these figures down, month by month, year after year, through the year 2003. I didn't give myself any raises; I treated the situation as though I would never make more than $40,000 a year.

An interesting thing happened. When I played this scenario out to the year 2003, I found I would have more than $2 million in cash with this simple savings plan! I thought to myself that if I did only half as well as my projection, I would still be in great shape, and certainly better than if I had no plan at all.

Most of us will move in one of two circles for the rest of our lives. In one, we run around frantically working for money. In the other, money works for us. You will never make money work for you if you have no plan. Most people simply have no plan, and their resources get away from them. Don't let this be you.

Your Goals Will Teach You

Goal setting is important not for what you get at the end of the rainbow but for what it makes of you in the process. Your goals will help you learn things you didn't know about yourself and other people. (For this reason I always suggest that couples set goals together. Simply take out a blank sheet of paper and put together what I call your dream list.) To set your goals, relax and sit back in the comfort of your favorite chair and simply dream about the things you want. You must dream about doing something as if you knew for sure you could have it. Allow yourself this essential part of the process. You may want to listen to some relaxing music at this time.

After you've spent five to ten minutes dreaming, get your notepad and start writing down your goals. Don't analyze and judge them; just keep writing until you have fifty or more items. The goals can be as simple as cleaning out your garage or as challenging as becoming a state senator. The key is to get your thoughts on paper.

After this, go through and prioritize the items on your list. Then organize your goals so that you'll accomplish the most immediate ones first. You will have short-range, intermediate, and long-range goals augmented by the tasks you must perform daily to achieve them. Plan for the achievement of your goals in one-, three-, five-, ten-, or twenty-year segments.

I tend to be fanatical about goal setting because I know it works. My wife said, "I want to get pregnant before I get too old to have children." I said, "Boom! No problem." My wife and I set a goal to have a child. So I wrote down a goal in the fall of 1990 that read as follows: "We will have a healthy child in the fall of 1991. This goal will be completed by November 30, 1991." (My daughter was born on November 8, 1991.) Now, I realize this process had a lot to do with things other than simply setting goals, but please don't miss my point. Goals give your life direction and will help you crystallize your thoughts, your actions, and your future.

Your Goals Can Change

Don't feel as though your goals hold you hostage. They may change as your situation and your priorities change. My goals changed when I decided I no longer wanted to be an actor and opted instead for a business career. This doesn't mean you've failed. It simply means you have changed. Sometimes these changes will result in you accomplishing even larger goals or finding greater happiness with smaller ones.

Tony Dungy helped recruit me to the University of Minnesota. Tony has always been a very goal-oriented, dedicated person—which is one of the reasons why he became one of the top young coaches in professional football. When he became a coach, many started speculating about when he would become one of the rare black head coaches in the NFL—a thing that didn't even exist until Art Shell became head coach of the Los Angeles Raiders. Tony's name came up whenever a head-coaching job was mentioned, but no one made him an offer. I saw him at the health club and talked about this. I told him that if people knew him as well as I did, they would know that everyone else was a lot more worried about this than he was. He told me he was happy as a defensive coordinator and could continue in this position for the rest of his coaching career. "When the NFL is ready, I'm ready," he said. "I don't spend my time worrying about things I can't control." He said that when he got the job, he wanted it to be for all of the right reasons.

Here is an example of someone who found happiness and joy in what he was doing although he had not achieved what he ultimately wanted. His goals were not any smaller; they were just put into a different perspective, a healthy one that worked for him.

On January 22, 1996, after fifteen years as an assistant coach, Dungy became the head coach of the Tampa Bay Buccaneers and the third African-American to coach in the NFL. Tony represents what persistence and perseverance are all about. There's no doubt that he will make history as one of the most successful coaches in the league. He's that kind of a person. The key is to maintain balance by not worrying about the uncontrollable while definitely controlling the things you can.

CHAPTER 8
DISCOVERING YOUR CORE VALUES

Walk quietly and deliberately into the storm. Think peacefully so your thoughts will keep you warm. Stand at the helm of your heart's true desire. Discovery can lift your spirits so much higher. Move with purpose toward what makes your soul heal and gladden. Then witness yourself receiving the wonderful things that can happen! Peace be with you in every way. Patience will keep anxiety at bay! All honor comes from standing and daring to begin. Even when you fall and have to stand and start again.

—**Saunni Dais**

> *I found that values, for each person, were numerous. Therefore, I proposed to write my value names and to annex to each a short precept—which fully expressed the extent I gave to each meaning. I then arranged them in such a way as to facilitate acquisition of these virtues.*
>
> **—Benjamin Franklin**

Late on a Sunday night in 1988, I found myself lying in the middle of my living-room floor with my head hurting so badly it felt as if it were going to burst. This was much more than a typical headache. I had experienced the worst migraines from head-on collisions on the football field, but nothing had come close to this. I couldn't even hold my head up because that only intensified the pain. The pain went from my head down through my lower back and into my legs. I thought I was having a stroke.

All I could do was call my wife with a faint cry, like a wounded animal in distress. She bounded down the stairs to see what was wrong. As she helped me to my feet, I pleaded with her to get me to the hospital quickly. The pain increased with each step. I begged her to hurry as she sped through the lights on the way to Fairview Southdale Hospital. Once there, I was rushed in to see a doctor and kept in the hospital overnight.

After a battery of tests, I was diagnosed with a severe sinus and ear infection that could have killed me had we not taken action. Even more disturbing, during the EKG, the doctor noticed unusual patterns caused by extreme anxiety and stress. I thought, "How could this happen to me?" I was young, only thirty-three years old, and by most standards I seemed to have more outward success than most. I certainly had more than my background would have predicted.

The doctor told me he had seen this pattern in type A personalities before. Sometimes, after dealing with years of stress and anxiety, the body and mind take a vacation. He told me that whatever I was going after wasn't worth killing myself for, and I'd better back off and try to enjoy life more than I seemed to be.

I sat on the chair in his office, with my head hanging down. I knew in my heart he was right. I thought this was the kind of thing that happened to other people. Not me, the big, strong, macho ex–football player. But, here I was, stressed out and in an emotional struggle for survival.

I should have noticed the signs six months earlier. My thirty-third birthday should have been a time of great celebration. I was driving a Mercedes-Benz, lived in a beautiful new three-bedroom town house, owned more than $1 million in real estate, and had enough money in the bank to satisfy any immediate and future needs. But it was the worst birthday I've ever had. I struggled that entire day with stress and anxiety.

Why was I so unhappy? I found I didn't really know where I stood in my own mind. In my heart, I knew I'd never be happy until I learned to respect my own progress and give myself credit for my own accomplishments, no matter how big or small.

I had to, as you must, learn never to worry about what anyone else was doing or expected of me so much that I lost sight of my own crystal ball. We come into this world at different times, confront different challenges, and have varying degrees of advantages and disadvantages. Focus on your own business. Read and learn what you can from and about others, but write and live according to your own script. Most of the unhappiness many people experience comes from an obsession with comparison.

Never Compare Yourself to Anyone

The hook is your desire to be approved of by others. The bait is any kind of reward. The minute you go for the bait, the game is playing you. You are no longer playing the game. You become a victim.

—Laurence G. Boldt

You will never measure up when you place someone else on a pedestal ahead of yourself. I became a victim of the very same programming that helped create my success. I would read about people like Donald Trump, Adnan Khashoggi, and Warren Buffett and proclaim that what I had was nothing compared to these people. I'd read about the awesome success of people like Curt Carlson, Carl Pohlad, and Irwin Jacobs, and feel I wasn't even scratching the surface. I felt inadequate. I believed I could work as hard as humanly possible and still never be worth the kind of money these people were worth. This scared me.

The more I read about the Forbes 400, the more like a loser I felt. I found myself having panic attacks. The thought of how hard I would have to work to be worth $100 million didn't bother me. I felt I needed to find a vehicle to get me there, and it wasn't the great job I had at the time. My life was spiraling out of control.

I was tremendously out of balance. Money was my number one priority, and it was making me miserable. I had become a victim of the mad rush of that 1980s mentality: "Get as much as you can, while you can!" For about a year, I felt as though I was cracking up. There was so much coming at me so fast it was hard to ascertain what to take from the table of success and what to leave.

Every business magazine I read offered 1,001 different ways to go after the brass ring. I was stressed out trying to keep up with it all. Every time I read another Horatio Alger story, I would mentally throw whatever I was focusing on at the time into the Dumpster and start thinking about the latest new fad in franchising, direct mail, or telemarketing. I didn't realize that as long as I was making measurable progress in a reasonable amount of time, I was succeeding.

I have since found a much healthier perspective for myself. This experience taught me that to compare myself with anyone is wrong. Never compare yourself with anyone! You came here at a different time than others, and you will probably leave at a different time. Envy will blur your focus.

People often value the success of others without understanding the circumstances or price paid to achieve it. Why should you care in the first place? It has nothing to do with your life or success. There will always be people with more or less than you have. Life is not fair and never will be.

The thing I learned is to do the best I can with what I have. That has to be good enough. I learned I was a very ungrateful person at that stage—because I wasn't thankful for my blessings. I couldn't enjoy anything because I was always looking for the next thing.

A friend of mine told me something one day that really hurt my feelings, but I knew it was true. He said, "How sad it is for a man to awaken to a wonderful morning, walk in a beautiful garden, or look at a gorgeous sunset and not even notice." That was me, rushing through life in an effort to accumulate more, more, more. Everything I watched and read was about making money. I had no other interests. If my friends didn't serve a purpose toward that end, I distanced myself from them slowly but surely.

I knew I had to change before I destroyed my life and the friendships I had spent years building. I've learned to read about and respect the accomplishments of others only to the extent it helps me make distinctions about what's important, but not to the point where their successes or failures become objects of personal comparison for me.

The 1980s was a decade of greed, and I was a product of it. Ingratitude breeds unhappiness and despair. I look at some of the people who were my heroes at that time. Many of them will live the rest of their lives in shame. They have lost their integrity, which is something that can never be bought. All for the love of money! Some of those people will spend the rest of their lives in prison for their greed. Charles Keating, Ivan Boesky, Dennis Levine, and a host of others were idolized for their ability to make money. Now they find themselves in the hall of shame. They were out of balance, and this led them to become out of control.

Being a one-dimensional person will also cause you to lose perspective, because life is made up of so many different things. We need a system of values to help keep us on track. Ambition is good and greed is bad. Greed causes destruction and ruin. The love of anything to the point of obsession can cause problems in your life. Before you know it, you will find yourself spinning out of control.

Food for Thought

No man is an island, entire of itself; every man is a piece of the continent, a part of the main.

—John Donne

One of my heroes in American business was Reginald F. Lewis. He was the chairman and CEO of Beatrice. His $1.7 billion leveraged buyout of that company in 1987 was an unprecedented accomplishment for a black businessman. He went from a working-class neighborhood to Harvard and finally joined elite business circles. He was a brilliant businessman who knew what he wanted and how to get there. Over the years, I have collected just about every article ever written about him. He was, indeed, something special. His autobiography, *Why*

Should White Guys Have All the Fun?, told of his incredible drive, awesome determination, and how he pushed himself beyond what most people would consider humanly possible. He died in January 1993 from brain cancer, at the age of fifty.

Lewis's death had a profound affect on me. I wondered what part stress and anxiety may have played in his illness. I reflected on stories in his book about his fast-paced lifestyle and unbelievable travel schedule. I thought about how often he might have gone without the proper sleep or diet. The awesome demands of his own ambition had to have had an effect.

I'm not a doctor, but common sense tells me that a lifestyle that intense would have to lead to severe consequences. It is well known that stress and anxiety can leave you open to sickness and disease. It only seems reasonable that these factors played some part in the early departure of what I consider an American hero.

I'm learning to move through life with not only a sense of purpose and passion but also an understanding that life is made to be enjoyed. No matter how much you accumulate, it will be a pittance compared to the vast riches of the world. I needed to find that delicate balance that would allow me to achieve my goals and yet not sacrifice an emotionally healthy life.

Ambition has its place in life, but it must be harnessed if it is to serve rather than enslave us. A system of values will help you approach life with a sense of calm and serenity, knowing that everything must be balanced and must fit into its proper place and time.

What Are Your Values?

Values are the foundation of our character and of our confidence. A person who does not know what they stand for or what they should stand for will never enjoy true happiness and success.

—L. Lionel Kendrick

Your values are the things you should cherish most. They represent a set of principles, standards, or qualities you consider worthwhile or desirable. A well-developed system of values will keep you whole. It will help keep you out of trouble as you travel through life's maze.

The operative question in discovering your values is this: What's most important to you? That is, what's most important to you about marriage, children, insurance, career, education, health, religion, or anything else? Success is not determined by getting what you want but by wanting what you get. You must understand that getting there does not require you to sacrifice the things that will make you happy along the way. Sometimes you can go on for years pursuing a course of action you think will make you happy, only to feel emptiness at the end. Had you asked me a few years ago, before I discovered my own core values, what my number one value in life was, I would have told you it was money. I thought money was the most important thing until I had a chance to step back and think about it. Now it doesn't even make the top five. I sat down and began to analyze my life and my feelings toward it, creating what I call my own constitution.

There are two definitions to understand in the following: A *value* is what I deemed most important, and a *rule* is the behavior I must demonstrate in order to live in line with that value and remain consistent. The thing to keep in mind is that these are my values; I don't wish to impose them on you. You must take the time to sit down and calmly think about your own life and what's most important to you. Only then can you come to grips with your own system of values.

Desi's Values (My Constitution)

1. **God:** To be one with God and all of his creations.
   Rule: To be godlike in my thinking and deeds.

2. **Health:** To maximize my physical health in order to operate my body and mind at peak efficiency.
   Rule: To cherish my body and mind and treat them with cleanliness and moderation. To do nothing that would violate my health either mentally or physically.

3. **Family:** To maximize harmony and closeness in my family.
   Rule: To approach my family life with as much enthusiasm as I do my business. To nurture and empower my family relationships to be the best they can be. To make time for my family, achieving balance between work and family life.

4. Personal Development: This is the foundation of my life. The key to a better future is me. It's not what happens to me that determines the quality of my life but what I do about it that makes the difference. **Rule:** To make learning a lifelong journey. To always stretch beyond the norm for excellence—then the stretch becomes a natural way to operate. To read, study, and model excellence each day, realizing that it's not what I get but what I become that will make me happy. I will always invest in myself without hesitation.

5. Freedom: To have the ultimate power of choice free from the decisions of others. To spend the rest of my life doing the work I love—speaking! To make every day my day.
Rule: My thoughts, decisions, and actions must manifest this total freedom. The only power things have over me is the power I give them.

6. Integrity: To be honest and fair in my dealings with other people. To always seek a win-win solution to problems. To look not for who's right but for what's best.
Rule: To treat people with dignity, respect, and truth. To call things as they are and not as I want or wish them to be. To make people feel as though they are the most important people in the world.

7. Financial Independence: To be wealthy enough to amplify the governing values in my life. To have money work for me instead of me working for it. I deserve success and will have it in direct proportion to the value I deliver to the marketplace.
Rule: Always make saving a priority to create the foundation for freedom.

- Only look at long-term approaches with solid returns. (*No pie in the sky.*)

- Only take advice from those who are competent (through their own experience) to give it.

- Do not lose money. Maximize the power of accumulation through compounding.

- Do not speculate; invest!

- Eliminate consumer debt; maximize investment debt.

8. **Patience:** I will master this virtue as part of everything I do, realizing that patience is its own reward. It is a key to my lifelong success.
Rule: Direction is more important than speed. It takes time for things to develop. The bigger the goal, the more time required. I will exercise faith as the cornerstone of patience. Life is not a destination, it's a journey.

9. **Persistence:** I will succeed in my goals no matter how long it takes. My life has no limits in terms of what I can do.
Rule: I will never give up! Rejection only makes me feel stronger and teaches me to find new and better ways of doing things. I will never entertain the thought of quitting short of my goals.

> *I'd rather die on my feet than live on my knees!*
>
> **—James Brown**

10. **Mastery of Emotions:** I will master my emotions by continually exercising the power of focus.
Rule: I will focus my attention on the things I want. I will think positively and live my life with forgiveness, passion, and impact.

As I look at my list of values, I realize how important this list was to me at a turning point in my life. It was put together with a great deal of thought and soul-searching. I was forced to go deeper inside myself than I ever had before and make tough decisions. Which values would come first? Why? How would the hierarchy of my values affect my behavior and subsequently the results I got from life? All of these questions are part of the values discovery process. For example, when I placed God as my number one value, it caused me to think. This is not to say I'm perfect—I am not! But at the same time, I felt as though, no matter what, I would be a better person for trying to operate according to the standards set forth by the Word.

With my number two value of health, I asked myself if I was being selfish placing my own individual health ahead of my family in the hierarchy. I came to the conclusion that if I don't take care of myself, I won't be around long enough to take care of them.

> *Many a businessman feels himself the prisoner of the commodities he sells; he has a feeling of fraudulency about his product and a secret contempt for it. Most important of all, he hates himself, because he sees his life passing him by without making any sense beyond the momentary intoxication of success.*
>
> **—Eric Fromm**

I was also conflicted about my sixth and seventh values. My number six value used to be financial independence, with integrity holding the number seven slot. A friend of mine, Rick, and I went through a monthlong process where we helped each other create a list of our own personal core values. He asked me if I would sell drugs or steal to make money. I assured him I would never do anything illegal or unethical for financial gain. He suggested I consider moving my value of integrity ahead of financial independence. That way, whenever I need to make a financial decision, I will never sacrifice my integrity. By exchanging these values in my hierarchy, I will always make the right decision.

I promise you that this exercise will change your life. If you don't know what you value most in life and in what order, you will find yourself making decisions that may not be in your own long-term best interest. If I know your values, I know what motivates you. If I know what is most important to you, I can predict your behavior. By the same token, if you know what's most important to you, you can predict your behavior in any situation. Many people experience a great deal of misery because they don't have the ability to determine what's most important to them. They end up victims, and that's no way to live.

Financial independence is still an important value for me, but to control my desire for it, I found it necessary to give it a lower priority in order to experience peace. You may have to do the same in making your own list. You will learn more about yourself than you ever knew before. After people attend one of my LifeTime Management Seminars, they often write to tell me that the discovery of their core values was the most valuable part of the experience.

A Question of Values: How Inland Container Corporation Was Born

A man dreamed of becoming a high-ranking corporate executive and worked for years to reach his dream but could get no further than middle management. Then one day he was brought into the chairman's office and told that he was being promoted to senior vice president because of his performance and years of dedication to the company. The chairman also informed him that there was only one rule: There would be a meeting the next morning, and when the time came for a vote on several key issues, he was to vote as the chairman voted, no questions asked, no matter what. This was not open for negotiation.

The next morning before the meeting, the man went in to the chairman and resigned. When asked for an explanation, the man said he was not about to be a puppet for anyone, no matter how badly he wanted the job, because it was against his value system. When the man got home, his wife asked him what he was doing there so early. He told her he had good news and bad news. The good news was that he had finally gotten the job of his dreams. The bad news was he had quit!

The next morning as he sat reading the newspaper, there was a knock at his front door. It was three of the senior managers who worked at the company. They informed him they had also quit and wanted to work for him. He told them he appreciated their loyalty, but it would be hard to work for someone who didn't even have a job. That day, the four of them sat down around his dining-room table, and Inland Container Corporation was born. It has since become one of the most successful companies of its kind in the world.

Me and My Dad

It took my father many years before he was able to put his values in order. As I mentioned previously, he always worked like a demon to provide for his family. I suppose he worked so hard because he never had much growing up, and he overcompensated because of the fear that came from the memories of being poor.

There were many times when I needed him. Whether I wished he would take me to a movie or sit in the stands on Parents Day during football season, I always found myself alone. It would make me feel bad to see the parents of my teammates come into the locker room after the game and know there would be no one waiting for me. By the time he looked up, I was grown and out on my own. Before he knew it, all that time had passed. Fortunately, after many years he learned that money is not the most valuable thing on earth but a tool to be used to increase the quality of our lives. My father and I had a wonderful relationship, and I am grateful for that. He taught me something valuable about the priorities of life.

In your pursuit of money for the sake of what it can buy, be careful you don't sacrifice the things money can't buy. I have decided that I will be there for my children—that's important to me. When you're dying, few people will ask you how much money you made or how big your house was. The things that will matter most are family, a few close friends, and the people you touch along the way. Whether you are already a parent or are a parent-to-be, make sure you spend time with your family. The time passes so fast you won't believe it!

CHAPTER 9
LEARNING FROM LIFE'S LESSONS

*This event has cast upon my time
a shadow that follows me. It tugs
and certainly pushes the best
that always lives in me.
It pulls me toward the conception
of my dream. Destiny will have
its way, it would seem.
It fulfills me, not with doubt, but
with confidence that I'll triumph,
I'll win! It assures me that all
my glory will come from seizing
the opportunity to begin.
Today, all the fascination and
challenge of fulfilling my Dreams
are here at last! Better days are here
to carry me to a place where my
future and I shake hands, at last!*

—Saunni Dais

> *It is the chiefest point of happiness that a person is willing to be what they are.*
>
> **—Desiderius Erasmus**

The summer of 1987 was an exciting time for me: I had just gotten married, and I was working as a franchise manager for PepsiCo, Inc. But my ambition was to have my own business. After months of looking at different things, I finally found it. It was Rainbow Custom Window Fashions, a business that specialized in selling window treatments of all kinds, such as miniblinds, microblinds, vertical blinds, and balloon shades. And it had two stores to boot. When I thought about the number of windows in the Twin Cities, I began to salivate over all of the cash coming my way. I believed that this was a no-miss situation.

A thirty-two-year-old entrepreneur named Mel Buchta sold my wife and me the business. He wanted to get out of retail and focus on the facility he was building in his home to manufacture blinds. He wanted a very close relationship with the person who bought the business, as he wanted to use the two stores to get his product into the marketplace. He was going to give us pricing that would knock the competition out, and show us the ropes in running the business until we felt comfortable enough to fly solo. My wife, Sue, had been an interior decorator for more than ten years, so we all felt as though this business was a natural fit. We all looked forward to building a profitable business together.

Walking out of the closing was the most exhilarating feeling in the world. I had finally found my own business. It was profitable, with a seven-year track record, and a seller who would be our supplier. How could we lose? I had visions of appearing on the cover of *Entrepreneur Magazine* with a pair of sunglasses on. The headline would read, "Blind Ambition: How Desi Williamson Created a Multimillion-Dollar Empire by Looking at Windows." The sun was shining, and I felt as though I could walk on water. I thought, "A business of my own! Everyone should have the opportunity to feel what I'm feeling, just once!"

Mel Buchta was also excited. His wife was nine months pregnant with their second child—they had a two-year-old daughter as well—

and he wanted to spend more time at home; he was a real family man. He and Sue got along great, and he was relieved to find that we were people he could work with. This had motivated him to sell to us, as he'd wanted to sell the business to people he liked. He had found what he felt was the perfect combination.

That July 4th weekend, Mel went to Brainerd, Minnesota, for a weekend retreat. He wanted to get away and celebrate the sale of the business. You could feel the excitement in his voice. He was really looking forward to this trip.

When the weekend was over, I was ready to get going. I couldn't wait to talk to Mel and discuss getting this venture started. I got a phone call on Monday morning from Mel's wife. She was sobbing, and from the sound of her voice, I could tell she was exhausted from crying. He had apparently jumped off a dock headfirst into shallow water and had broken his neck. He was floating in the lake when they found him. I broke down and started to cry. When Sue came into the room, I told her, and she cried as well.

After hanging up the phone, we sat together in shock that something like this could happen. We were numb. We couldn't even think about the effect it would have on our lives from a business perspective because there were more important issues at hand. He had friends who would never see him again, and a wife who would have to raise two children alone.

After the funeral was over, the reality of running the business without any direction set in. We were horrified! I had talked Sue into giving up a secure job she'd had for ten years with a well-known company in the interior-design business. She had given up benefits and retirement plans.

The two stores were on opposite ends of town. One was in Golden Valley, Minnesota, a suburb about ten minutes from our home in Edina, and the other was in Apple Valley, which seemed like a world away. The Apple Valley store was in a small dying strip mall. I knew that if we were to have any chance of surviving, we needed more foot traffic. I decided to move to a larger mall, but there was a major risk. The mall had more traffic, but the rent was three times as much as we were paying.

We made the move anyway. This mall had strong anchor tenants and we had an ironclad, four-year lease with an exclusivity clause. Our space was well located in the mall, and we went on to invest some

$20,000 in leasehold improvements. Things looked promising. Our first full year in the business, despite losing Mel, we made a small profit and were able to pay Sue a salary. We felt great!

In the spring of the following year, we learned that the mall was going to get a much stronger anchor tenant, Budget Power. We knew the name well. It was owned by a $100 million company called Thompson Enterprises. They were strong, and even though they sold ready-made blinds, we felt no threat because our products were all custom-made. Our customers paid 50 percent down when placing an order, and the balance on installation. We knew Budget Power had the ability to draw, and the fact that we were less than fifty yards from them could do us nothing but good. Our sales continued to climb over the summer as Budget Power moved in and got themselves accustomed to doing business in Apple Valley. We relished the thought of having people come into our store to compare the difference between ready-made blinds and custom. Our exclusivity agreement protected us against competitive activity in custom window treatments, and life was good.

In the fall, things changed. I noticed that our sales were starting to slump miserably. I couldn't figure out why. It's one thing to be off 10 or 20 percent, but when you go down 30 and 40 percent, you'd better apply a tourniquet fast, before you bleed to death. I decided to visit Budget Power and was shocked. They had almost an exact replica of my store inside of theirs and were selling at my cost. Because of their huge volume purchases, they could buy at better discounts and were ripping us to shreds. To make matters worse, the people we'd hired to manage our store would often not show up on time or at all. Some stole from us, and others just didn't care.

Our volume hit the skids. We had to close the Golden Valley store and put our focus on the Apple Valley location, because we had a larger financial commitment there and it had the most potential. But each month volume went down further.

It got so bad that Sue would come home with a horrified look on her face. I knew immediately that this meant more money would be needed to cover our monthly expenses. For three months, I drained our personal savings to meet our monthly debts. I've never felt so helpless and desperate in my life. We had more sleepless nights than I care to mention.

I was finally forced to deal with the man who owned the mall. My store was dying. I let him know how furious I was that he had breached our contract by allowing the big corporate conglomerate to come in and ruin my business. I told him I would no longer pay him rent as long as Budget Power was allowed to sell the same products at my cost. He told me that if I breached the lease, he would sue me for the balance, which, for three more years, totaled $30,000.

I was sick to my stomach. Everything I had worked for up to that point was going down the drain. Besides running the business, we still had a household to support, with mortgage payments, car payments, and all the things associated with living. I also had a real estate business and a full-time job at PepsiCo, a very demanding company in a competitive industry.

I felt as though I was losing my grip but was determined to keep my job, the one thing that gave us any security. Each day, as I reported to work, I offered a giant smile and pleasant attitude that masked the turmoil inside of me.

I had to take drastic action, and soon. It was only a matter of time before my bank account would dry up. I listed our house and started the process necessary to sell it. I was more than $100,000 in debt and was bleeding badly. I hired a lawyer, who told me my situation didn't look good. The mall owner was worth millions and could drain me dry if I tried to sue him for breach of the lease. Our lawyer told me he would be willing to take my money if I chose to pursue litigation, but he said it might be necessary to cut off the arm in order to save the body. He advised me to close the business and negotiate with the owner on a settlement that would terminate our agreement. He said he could buy me some time through written communications with the mall owner's lawyer and by sending a demand letter with the threat of a lawsuit that would never be carried out. This bought me ninety days.

We went back and forth. Finally the mall owner felt sorry for me and let me out of the agreement for $3,000. I was able to pay this over the next ninety days. I found out later that he had agreed to this settlement because he had already found a tenant who was to move in at the end of the ninety days and enjoy the fruits of the time and effort my wife and I had put into this store. We felt as though we were losing a child. We cried the day we sold our countertops, our chairs, and the other equipment we'd bought just months earlier. At least we were done with this episode. But there was still the problem of the bank and my $100,000 debt.

We began to think about what we could do to pay off what seemed to be a Mount Everest of debt. The only place to look was to the real estate we owned. The piece of property with the most promise was our house. Fortunately, we had bought a small house on a quarter-acre lot in a very desirable part of town and had improved it over the years. It was worth more than $300,000, and we owed only $108,000 against it. I had a strong relationship with a banker who was willing to loan me 80 percent of the value, about $240,000, more than enough to pay off the bank and protect our credit rating. We would have a much higher mortgage payment, but that seemed insignificant compared to having a $100,000 albatross around our necks. Luckily, interest rates then hit a twenty-year low, and we were able to secure a rate of 7 percent, which put our mortgage payment back to what it was before we'd had to borrow the extra money.

The whole situation was anything but funny at the time, but I can honestly say that I can now look back and laugh. This was one of the best things that ever happened to me. It taught me that when life knocks me down, I have to get up. If it keeps knocking me down, I have to keep getting up, again, again, and again! I also learned that there's nothing that can't be overcome with enough faith and tenacity. The only way to fail is to quit.

Today, I'm grateful for this failure. It gave me a depth of understanding about myself and other people I otherwise would never have possessed. It made me a wiser person and set me up to earn far more in future ventures because I would approach each situation with more savvy.

Whatever you're faced with in life—a failed relationship or business, the loss of a loved one, or a huge financial setback—know none of these situations are greater than your ability to overcome them. This faith will give you the power to move beyond or through obstacles to reach your ultimate decision.

She Wanted to Live

My grandmother is the strongest person I have ever known. She is a woman of extremely high character and moral fiber. At ninety-three years old, she lives alone and takes care of herself despite the pain of arthritis and respiratory problems. Each day she rises before 7:00 A.M., puts on her makeup, and gets dressed as though she's going to work.

She suffered a stroke one night and, reaching for the phone, noticed it wasn't in its usual place on the right side of her bed. She was gasping for breath when she stood up to find it. She fell to the floor in pain and remembered the phone was on the opposite side of her bed, where she had placed it earlier. She later told me she crawled to the other side of the bed and dialed 911, and then called my father to come and get her. The ambulance beat my father to the house, and my grandmother had crawled to the door and was waiting for them when they knocked.

I knew something was wrong when I called her that Monday night and there was no answer. She's always home in the evening unless she's out of town, and I always know when that is. It upsets me when I call and she is ill but hasn't told me. She doesn't want me to worry, she says. My grandmother later told me she never entertained the idea of dying as she was crawling toward that phone to call 911 and then to the door. She said it took everything inside of her to drag her 220-pound body around that house in the dark. All she could think about was getting up. She said me, her children, her grandchildren and her great-grandchildren were the things that kept her alive.

When life knocks you down, get up! If my ninety-three-year-old grandmother can do it, what's my excuse? What's yours? There is none. If you can look up, you can get up!

You've Got to Be Bold

I have a cousin named V.S. who gives a whole new meaning to the word *cheap*. His idea of fine dining is a bucket of fish and chips from Long John Silver's. He's a wealthy man with incredible savings habits. On a winter night a few years ago, we were traveling in separate cars on a trip from Los Angeles to St. Louis when we found ourselves stranded by snow in the mountains a few miles past Williams, Arizona. State troopers would not let us go any farther and were turning people around on the freeway. We were forced to go back to Williams to find a place to bed down for the night.

One family seemed to own everything in town, including the gas station, the convenience store, and the only motel. It was snowing so hard we could barely see two feet in front of us. We asked if there were any rooms and were told there was only one left. The owner said she and her husband would give us a ten-dollar discount off the forty-dollar rate because the room had shortcomings. It sounded great until we got to the room. It had no bed, television, phone, or heat. She threw us a couple of blankets, two pillows, asked us for thirty dollars, and said good night. We huddled together on that cold floor and attempted to fall asleep, hoping morning would come soon. At 3:00 A.M., my cousin jumped up from what appeared to be a dead sleep, got his coat, and headed for the door. When I asked him where he was going, he shouted, "I'm going to get some of my damn money back!"

The couple lived on the premises in a small house. You could hear my cousin, for probably a mile, banging on the door in the blinding snowstorm. A few minutes later, he emerged from the elements with cash in hand. He had two ten-dollar bills. He gave me one of them, stuffed the other in his hip pocket, climbed back underneath the blankets on that cold floor, and fell fast asleep, as if to say, "Now I can get a good night's sleep!" Ten dollars seemed to be adequate for such a room.

I've been laughing from that day to this one. I still can't believe anyone could be that bold. What he did took guts. I imagine they weren't often awoken by a black man in the middle of the mountains, in a blinding snowstorm, at 3:00 A.M. I still tease my cousin about this cross-country mishap every time I see him, and we get a big laugh out of it.

His action taught me that boldness has its place in life. Anytime something happens that violates your values, you can't just let it slide—that will only teach you to compromise in other areas of your life. You will discover things about yourself you never knew were possible when you do something bold. Sometimes it is not enough to merely knock on a door. Sometimes you've got to knock it down.

Pay Attention to Wake-up Calls

Never for a moment do we lay aside our mistrust of the ideals established by society, and of the convictions which are kept by it in circulation. We always know society is full of folly and will deceive us in the matter of humanity. It is an unreliable horse, and blind into the bargain. Woe to the driver, if he falls asleep!

—Albert Schweitzer

One warm summer night at 2:30 A.M., I was sitting in my car half asleep, waiting for a friend who'd gone into a restaurant to order something to eat after we'd attended a party. The window was rolled down. I was caught completely off guard when I felt the cold barrel of a .357 Magnum crash against my temple. The assailant hit me in the head twice with the gun, walked around to the passenger's side, climbed into the car, and told me to drive. As I drove this man around town with the gun pointed at my gut, I knew he could very well kill me anytime; I knew him. His name was Lucky, and he was known all over St. Louis as a ruthless person who had killed people and gotten away with it. I had briefly attended elementary school with him, and even then he was known as a crazy person who would do anything on a dare.

This death journey went on for ninety minutes before he jumped out of the car and very casually said, "Later!" He assured me that if I reported this occurrence to anyone, I would end up dead, and I knew he meant it. I went home, jumped under the covers, and shook in terror the rest of the night.

This was a wake-up call. Had I been more aware that night, this possibly would not have happened. I had lost track of the kind of neighborhood I was in; it was certainly no place to fall asleep in my car in the wee hours of the morning. That day, I learned to pay attention to everything around me at all times. Unfortunately, a few years later Lucky would be shot in the head, falling prey to the same misery he'd heaped upon others. I'd had my wake-up call, but he had never paid any attention to his. It cost him his life.

If you've ever been daydreaming while driving and suddenly found yourself slamming on your brakes, only to stop a few feet short of the car in front of you, that's a wake-up call! A negative performance review in your job is a wake-up call. Bad feelings in a relationship that erupt into harsh arguments are wake-up calls. Lagging sales and the resignations of key people in your business are wake-up calls that tell you to take stock and change your management style before it's too late.

Each day of our lives we get wake-up calls, yet few people are smart enough to stop, take a deep breath, and learn from these incidents. The person who slams on their brakes inches from an auto collision and then continues to drive like a person possessed until finally they end up dead or killing someone else did not heed their wake-up call.

Jewel's Lament

There was a kid who grew up across the street from me in St. Louis named Jewel Meeks. He was loud and always talked back to adults and anyone else who crossed his path. He was disrespectful to just about everyone he met. He picked fights just for fun, because he knew most people he challenged would back down. His five brothers were also all eager to fight anyplace, anytime. Jewel often caused fights between his brothers and others. He thought he was really doing something. I always found the best course of action was to avoid him completely. Everyone in the neighborhood felt that way. Jewel had many wake-up calls but never paid any attention.

One day he was visiting another neighborhood and walked across the lawn of an elderly man who was known to be nice but no one to fool with. Jewel walked all over the man's property, talking loud and using all kinds of profane language.

There's a belief where I grew up that you should give older people their respect, especially older men. Old men who end up with anything in life have gone through hell and back to get it. They will take you out of the game if you try to take advantage of them, and they are not about to tolerate abuse from some smart-mouthed kid.

The old man told Jewel he would appreciate it if he would get off his property and curtail the use of profanity in his presence. Jewel told him what he and his brothers were going to do to him. The old man asked Jewel again to leave the property. Jewel was steadfast, all the while hurling obscenities. The old man went inside, came back with a revolver, and shot Jewel dead. No one was surprised.

Certainly, the old man was wrong for the course of action he took.

Murdering someone is not the correct way to resolve conflict. That didn't make any difference to Jewel. Had he paid attention to many of the wake-up calls he had along the way, he might still be alive today.

I dated a pretty girl one summer who lived across the street from me and a few houses down the street from Jewel. Her name was Emily. Throughout elementary school, when I liked her, she didn't like me; when she decided to like me, I didn't like her. We started to go out in high school. She was always attracted to thuggish, gangster types. That summer, her boyfriend was in jail. He sent a message to the streets that anyone messing with her was dead meat when he got out of the joint. Wake-up call! Needless to say, I immediately ended the relationship.

I was on vacation in St. Louis one fall day and happened to be driving home from my father's restaurant to get some much-needed rest. It was one of those dark, rainy, overcast days when the only thought on my mind was to get home, lie down, and forget about things for a while. So I wasn't in any hurry, taking my time along a route I'd driven a thousand times before in my life. I was having some pleasant thoughts as I drove past Fairgrounds Park, a landmark in inner-city St. Louis. I'd played Little League baseball and football in that park. It was there the whole dream that led to a football scholarship at the University of Minnesota had gotten started.

Though daydreaming, I was very conscious of my driving because of the cold rain falling that day. I was driving twenty-five miles per hour in a thirty-five-miles-an-hour zone. They'd trained us in driver's ed to watch out for the other guy, and I was clearly doing that. As I approached an intersection, I noticed a car coming toward me in the opposite lane. The next thing I knew, this car was attempting to turn left without stopping at the stop sign. As he turned toward me, I braced myself and spun my wheel hard to the right in an effort to avoid him, but could not. As I readied for the crash, I saw my wife, my seven-month-old son, my three-year-old daughter, my father, my mother, and my beloved grandmother. I thought I might never see them again. My heart raced. I saw death staring me in the face and could not get out of the way. The impact turned my car around 180 degrees. My head hit the dashboard, and my body twisted like a pretzel. There was smoke and steam everywhere.

When I regained consciousness, I was lying in the emergency room. Wake-up call! It dawned on me at that point that no matter how quick, well prepared, or defensive you are, there are some things you can't anticipate. Life can still catch you on the blind side. Sometimes life will force you to deal with it right at the point of impact. That's why it's so important to approach life with a grateful mind. All too quickly, it can be taken away by something as simple as the turning of a steering wheel by a good person who happens to be heading in the wrong direction at the wrong time.

Sometimes it takes drastic circumstances for us to realize how precious life is. The key is to recognize ahead of time how valuable the gift of life is. In my emergency, the things I feared most were never holding my children again, not seeing them grow up, not telling my wife how much I love her, not letting my father and mother know, one more time, how much I love them, and not being able to tell my grandmother again how much I appreciate her for believing in me. I was given another chance, to live, to love, to make a difference.

Many of us die each day because we don't pay attention to the subtle clues that something is out of whack. The next time something happens in your life that represents a wake-up call, stop, take a deep breath, slow down, and ask yourself, "What is the message in this?" If you really take the time to think about it, you will find the answer. Don't ignore knocks on your door. Don't be someone who continually beats their head against the wall, making the same dumb mistakes again and again. This is a form of insanity that, if continued, can only take you down. From this day forward, keep your antennae up, and heed your wake-up calls.

Save Your Money

Too many people spend money they haven't earned, to buy things they don't want, to impress people they don't like.

—**Will Rogers**

The average person spends a lot more than they make. In order to really take control of your life, you must take control of your finances. This means you must learn to pay yourself first! This sounds simple, and it is, if you are willing to make a real commitment. I don't care how much money you earn, if you don't have a plan for it, you will find it slipping through your fingers and you'll end up flat broke. Gaining financial security doesn't involve some kind of magical formula. Getting control of your finances involves the following basic principles:

Pay Yourself First: Over the last twenty years I've been able to save more than 25 percent of what I earned each year. My good fortune came about only with the discipline to sacrifice immediate gratification to gain greater freedom later on. I don't care how much or little you earn; it's what you do with it that counts. If someone else has to wait, make them wait, but always, always, make the first payment to You, Inc. With persistence, you will develop a healthy nest egg that will start you on the pathway to freedom.

Learn to Live on Less Than You Earn: Learn to allocate your money to best serve your personal interests.

- Learn to live on 60 percent of your income.

- Learn to use 10 percent for tithing to whatever cause you believe in.

- Learn to use 10 percent for capital creation.

- Learn to use 10 percent to invest in your future.

- Learn to invest 10 percent in your own personal growth and development.

If you want to accelerate your progress, learn to live off even less of your income. Imagine what would happen if you could live off 40 percent of your income. You would then have another 20 percent available for investments. If you could really tighten your belt and live off 30 percent of your income, you would have an additional 30 percent to invest in buying your freedom. You might be feeling a bit of discomfort about the thought of living off such a small amount, but remember our lessons from the previous chapters. If you really want to achieve anything of significance, you've got to be willing to do some things differently and possibly be uncomfortable. If you're not, you will keep getting the same old results.

If you aren't making as much money as you'd like, there are many ways to invest or start your own business for a small amount of money.

It's amazing: There are opportunities everywhere if you just take the time to investigate them. Network marketing is one of the most powerful vehicles in the country, and it is making more millionaires of people more quickly than any other business: Nutrition for Life, Excel, Amway, Mary Kay, Herbalife, and Shaklee are just a few. The key is to find one that works for you. But again, this will require an investment of time and energy on your part.

If you develop enough savvy to save a sizable nest egg, you will find the right places to put it if you surround yourself with the right people. You can't invest what you don't have!

I see so many people in financial straits, and it affects every other area of their lives. *The Richest Man in Babylon,* by George S. Clason, is a wonderful book that should be required reading for everyone. It profiles the story of a wealthy man named Algamish, who had taken a particular interest in a young scribe by the name of Arkad. The young scribe was interested in how Algamish had become so wealthy. The old man explained that the way he became wealthy was by religiously practicing a simple principle: "A part of all you earn is yours to keep!" After suffering a series of setbacks over a period of years, Arkad would eventually take the place of Algamish as the Richest Man in Babylon and express the same principles.

You, too, can achieve financial independence if you are willing to invest in yourself. I paid $1.95 for Clason's book twenty years ago. It has been responsible for my making many thousands of dollars and achieving a level of financial independence I never thought possible.

Build Yourself a Mastermind Group

In Napolean Hill's classic book *Think and Grow Rich,* he talks about the power of having a mastermind group. This is a group of like-minded people who can help you reach your dreams. You must find a group of people with different skills who you can meet with frequently to help you in your quest for success. You must also bring a contribution to the group. The group size should be limited to somewhere between seven and a dozen people. The more diverse their backgrounds, the better. You need people who think differently from you, who can give you honest feedback about your goals and progress, and who will also encourage you to stretch beyond your limits.

I can't stress the power of a group like this enough. My mastermind group consists of people who are smarter than I am in different areas, such as real estate, financial planning, marketing, and investing. My relationship with these individuals has allowed me to make quantum leaps in both my personal and my professional progress.

I'm light-years ahead of where I would be had we not put together this group. I also bring sales, marketing, consulting, and speaking expertise to the group. We all help one another get where we want to go at a much faster rate than we would by ourselves. When putting together your mastermind group, make sure you involve yourself with people who will challenge you. So often, we are afraid we will alienate friends by wanting to associate with people who will stretch us. Old friends will say we've changed now that we've made it. The reality is they may not have changed. That's their problem, not yours.

If you want to be successful, be around people who are, or who have at least made a commitment to be something more than they are. This will have a dramatic and immediate impact on your life. When several like minds are brought together, a larger, more intelligent force is born. This is vitally important, particularly in the area of finance and investing. You need to develop a team of experts in the areas of insurance, tax planning, financial planning, estate planning, real estate, and investing. The old saying is true: "Once the mind is stretched by a new idea, it can never return to its original dimensions."

You've Got to Sell Yourself!

You are the first thing sold in any proposition that involves the exchange of value between two or more people. I've seen many situations where people didn't get the job or the sale they were after because they didn't understand self-promotion. You're always selling, no matter what. I often have people tell me they are not involved in selling because they are a nurse, doctor, lawyer, or schoolteacher.

You are selling health-care services as a nurse or doctor, your ability to get results for your clients as a lawyer, and ideas and education if you're a schoolteacher. If you're going to be exceptional in any walk of life, you're going to have to be good at letting people know what you bring to the table. Why should you have the job, get the promotion, or get the business instead of someone else? Unless you can convince them that your USP (unique selling proposition) provides them with greater benefits than the others, you will not get the results. Your unique selling proposition involves what you can do for someone else that they cannot do for themselves. What service do you provide that can add value to what they're doing? Your USP must involve the specific expertise you possess that someone else would be willing to pay for.

This core expertise involves continued education. You must find the classes, seminars, and books that can help you develop the expertise that will distinguish you from every other wanna-be who is going after the same thing you are. You must be able to communicate this in less than thirty seconds.

Write your unique selling proposition. After you've crafted your USP, hone it to the point where you can recite it in thirty seconds or less. I suggest you use pencil in case you want to make changes later.

What Are You Selling?

Many people don't succeed because they don't understand the difference between features and benefits. This is true no matter what they're selling, especially when it's themselves! A feature is what something is; a benefit is what it does. This is the reason why most résumés end up in the scrap heap. They are filled with useless information about the prospective candidate instead of the results that can be derived for the company by hiring them. Applicants then blame the company or fate when they continue to get rejected, instead of taking a look at themselves. You must market yourself continually no matter how successful you currently are. People have short memories, and you have to ensure that you will continue to occupy and command your SOM (share of mind).

Back in 1979, I was hired as a sales representative for Johnson & Johnson. I was working for McNeil Consumer Products Company, which sold Tylenol. While driving through my territory one day, I considered the marketing and sales manual they had so beautifully constructed. I thought what an advantage it would be to have a similar document featuring me as the major product.

From that day, I began to collect and file documentation on everything I did. This included letters of recommendation, sales reports, results from sales contests, awards, and any other information that would highlight the benefits that one could derive from a professional association with me. I organized this information in a portfolio in chronological order, and took it with me on every job interview from that point forward. When a prospective employer asked for a documented track record, I had one! I've had some great jobs during my career, but none of them were dropped in my lap. My preparations would blow some interviewers away. Some would be so insecure that this would scare them, particularly if they were to be my boss. They figured that sooner or later, a person with this kind of foresight would be after their job. I didn't want to work for anyone like that, anyway. My portfolio helped eliminate companies I didn't want to work for as much as it helped me get hired by some great ones.

You've got to learn how to market and sell yourself if you really want to succeed in this world. Just like any other product, you've got to remake yourself every few years with new packaging and updated skills. You must continue to become new and improved.

Do What You Fear Most First!

Our doubts are traitors,
And make us lose the good we oft might win,
By fearing to attempt.

—Shakespeare

You may sometimes be paralyzed by fear. I've found that the best way to overcome fear is to do what scares you most first. Whether it's public speaking or a fear of water, heights, or anything else, the best way to confront these fears is head-on.

For instance, I've always had a terrible fear of water. When a good friend of mine asked me to go water-skiing a few years ago, I told him he was nuts! He worked on me for about three weeks. Finally, I agreed to go, as long as I could wear at least two life jackets. Once I was able to get up on those skis, I had the time of my life. I couldn't believe I was on a lake going thirty miles per hour on a couple of planks. I'd never for a minute thought that I would enjoy this experience, but afterward, I couldn't wait to get out there again.

You will often find the same thing to be true. Whatever it is you are afraid of, just do it without worrying about the outcome. You will find that your fear will diminish after you discover that those gremlins were only figments of your imagination.

Victor, the Wrestling Bear

Whenever I find myself racked with fear, I'll remember the time I wrestled a bear. Often the challenge at hand will then pale in comparison, for few of the challenges I've faced stood eight feet, three inches and weighed a quarter of a ton. I wrestled him as part of a promotion for a health club I worked at during my summers off in St. Louis. I was in great shape and was excited about the opportunity to wrestle this bear—until the day of the event. It was 98 degrees outside with 98 percent humidity, and Victor was not in a good mood. I went to get a look at Victor before the match. I thought to myself, "I must be out of my mind!" Hundreds of people outside were waiting to see three football players—two from the pros and myself, a college football player—tussle with this bear. I would be the first.

When I climbed into the ring, Victor was on all fours, rocking back and forth. My heart was beating a thousand miles a minute. When the trainer clapped his hands, Victor stood up on his hind legs. The man clapped his hands again, and Victor moved into action. He threw me around that ring like a rag doll, and what turned out to be two minutes seemed like two hours. Finally, Victor got tired of toying with me, and on a final command from his trainer, pinned me to the mat and began to lick me all over through his muzzle.

When the next guy tried to get into the ring, Victor went after him with a vengeance. He was not playing this time. He was angry. His trainer jumped into the ring and popped Victor in the nose with a right cross. The bear fell to his knees. The trainer then grabbed the microphone and explained to the crowd that he and Victor had had a little misunderstanding and everything was okay now.

I learned a great deal about fear that day. Courage is not the absence of fear but the mastery of it. It's okay to be fearful. It's a normal emotional reaction. Just don't let it stop you from taking action. Do what you're going to do in spite of the fear. Take action anyway! As I think back, had I not taken advantage of the opportunity

to wrestle this bear, I would have regretted it for the rest of my life.
I would have always wondered what it was like.

Don't let fear cheat you out of the opportunity to learn something
new or something more about yourself than you knew before. That's
where the juice of life flows.

It Pays to Be Nice!

I once missed a flight because my daughter was sick with the flu.
I wanted to redeem the unused ticket, but according to their rules,
I had to be the sick one. I spent forty-five minutes in a heated debate
with the reservations staff. When I wanted to exchange the ticket for
another flight, I became frustrated and asked to speak to a supervisor.
A huge guy with a thick mustache lumbered over to the counter.
I asked him if he had the authority to make a decision in this regard.
He responded by quipping, "I can do anything I want to." I explained to
him that I was a frequent flier with more than three-quarters of
a million miles to my credit. Then I hit him with the bomb. I asked, "Sir,
if you could help me in this situation, why wouldn't you?" He stopped
dead in his tracks for what seemed like thirty seconds, then proceeded
to verify my frequent-flier status and give me a new ticket to the city of
my choice.

This situation once again reinforced my belief that it pays to be
nice. I could have lost my temper, exploded, and exacerbated the
entire situation, but this would not have brought me the result I was
looking for. You will find that this discipline will pay dividends more
often than not in every aspect of your life.

Even if you have to deliver bad news, there is a correct way to do
it. I once left my car running with the radio on while I ran a short
errand. The radio was louder than normal because I had ejected a cas-
sette tape. It was the middle of the winter, so both windows were
rolled up. As I returned to the car and opened the door to get in, an old
man came up and read me the riot act. He screamed at me, saying he
could hear my music as he was getting in his car and I was causing
noise pollution.

A few years ago, I would have told him in no short order where to
get off. Because I've changed my ways and learned to be nicer, I simply
paused and listened to the old man. I then very nicely explained to him

that he should mind his own business and said I didn't want him to get hurt in the future. I told him he didn't know me from Adam, and some people might not take kindly to his getting so personal with them. I also mentioned that people have gotten killed for less. After I explained this to the gentleman, he actually thought about it for a minute and thanked me. I was in shock. I smiled as I got into my car. What could have been an inflammatory situation turned out fine. It always pays to be nice.

CHAPTER 10
TWELVE LIFE-CHANGING PRINCIPLES

Reaffirmed

*My Soul doth resonate and
the world can feel the vibration
of my thunder.*

*My spirit is resilient, like a
cockroach, it's a natural wonder.*

*My mind sings a song
as sweet as an angel's.*

*My principles are rigid lest they
are bent to positive angles.*

—Saunni Dais

> *Every individual has a place to fill in the world and is important in some respect, whether he chooses to be so or not.*
>
> **—Nathaniel Hawthorne**

I've discovered that life really does come full circle if you meet it halfway. There are many principles you must master in order to get off your assets and make your life work the way you want it to. I want to give you what I believe to be some of the most powerful ones. These, combined with my own list of core values, have helped to center and balance my life. What follows is by no means all-inclusive, but it will give you the framework to jump-start your life.

The Principle of Self-Belief

> *One comes to be of just such staff as that on which the mind is set.*
>
> **—Upanishads**

This is a feeling of certainty about the outcome of something. You must learn to believe in yourself, because if you don't, nobody else will. Doubt will almost always creep in and try to wreck your plans. You cannot afford to leave it up to someone else to get you started.

Sometimes life moves much more slowly than we want it to. Sometimes you want something so much you can taste it, but it seems so far away. I say, "Hold fast to your goal and continue to believe in yourself as long as you have breath. You never know when your time will come." Tony Dungy said he knew one day he would get his chance to coach in the National Football League. He was prepared to continue to dream about and work toward that end, no matter how long it took. You must do the same thing. You can make it! Don't ever give up, especially on you.

The Principle of Faith

Be patient toward all that is unresolved in your heart
And try to love the questions themselves.

—Rainer Maria Rilke

F aith is believing in yourself until you succeed. Anyone can exercise faith when things are going well. It's when you hit those bumps in the road that your faith will be tested. You will no doubt become sad, mad, depressed, worried, and frustrated during your journey to self-actualization. You need to be aware of these emotions, both consciously and subconsciously. There's an old Chinese proverb that says, "Even a hurricane only lasts a day." The Chinese bamboo tree can shoot up as much as ninety feet in a matter of weeks. Such growth occurs only after five to ten years of good conditions. This is called "the Process." The tree doesn't really grow that tall in a matter of weeks. The care and nurturing it receives up to that point allows it to reach its maximum potential.

Your life is the same way. You must continue to nurture your dreams for as long as it takes you to reach them. Your faith in a higher power and yourself will help you weather bad circumstances. Just don't give up!

Our demons are our own limitations, which shut us off from the realization of the ubiquity of the spirit. . . . Each of these demons is conquered in a vision quest.

—Joseph Campbell

Everything in life is temporary, as is life itself. When you leave this earth, you'll be dead for a lot longer than you were ever alive. Why not give yourself every chance to succeed? As long as you have breath in your body, you're still in the game. Just believe in yourself long enough, and you will eventually get where you want to go.

The Principle of Self-Love

Thoroughly to know oneself, is above all art, for it is the highest art.

—Theologia Germanica

You can't love anyone else until you first love you. Many people are looking for love in all the wrong places instead of first looking inside of themselves for the emotional support they need.

I know a guy named Glenn. He's sixty-two years old and has a body like Adonis. He walks with a swagger and an air of confidence that speaks not of arrogance but of self-love. I once asked him what caused him to have such an incredible outlook on life. He told me to imagine being involved in an incredible love affair, the kind where you can't wait to see the other person. When you think of them, you get goose bumps. You can get through almost any difficulties you may encounter during the day, as long as you know you will get to see this person at the end of it. The very thought of this person makes you excited about your life.

He then marched me over to a mirror and told me to look into it. He told me to imagine that the person I was having this mad love affair with was myself; this was his secret.

He said it had taken him years to come to grips with this self-love concept. He had been through two marriages and raised three kids before he learned about it. He said when you learn to love yourself, life takes on a whole new glow. You wake up each day excited! People want to be around you because they want some of that to rub off on them. It's not about arrogance. Arrogance involves an outward display of emotion that usually centers on trying to impress or belittle someone else in order to make yourself look good.

Self-love is an internal thing. It comes from the inside out rather than the outside in. The key is to recognize the fact that you are enough to make you happy. If you base your happiness on people or things other than you, you will more than likely be crushed when they don't meet your expectations. Keep the focus on you and what you can do on a continual basis to make yourself happy.

The Principle of Persistence

> *Anyone who proposes to do good must not expect people to roll stones out of his way, but must accept his lot calmly, even if they roll a few more upon it.*
>
> **—Albert Schweitzer**

Persistence is the one thing that will definitely make the difference in whether you will reach your goals and live your dreams. Remember, the only way you can ever fail in life is to quit. As long as you keep trying, you are a winner. No matter how well prepared or talented you are, be ready to have doors slammed in your face. No matter how well received you are, there will always be someone who doesn't like you. One thing is for sure: If you give up without giving yourself every chance to win for as long as you can, you will fail.

Michael Jordan was cut from the basketball team during his sophomore year in high school. Who would have thought, at the time, that he would go on to be, without question, the greatest basketball player in the history of the game? I recently saw a program that profiled Michael Jordan's life, and it was interesting to listen to his high school basketball coach try to justify his reason for cutting the greatest basketball player in the world. Michael didn't give up, thank goodness. Think of what we would all have missed.

I've had to go through the same things in my life and so will you. Expect it, accept it, and deal with it! If you quit, you will be cheating the world as well as yourself out of receiving the gift only you can give.

The Principle of Proactivity

All labor that uplifts humanity has dignity and importance and should be undertaken with painstaking excellence.

—Dr. Martin Luther King Jr.

This is the fifth skill necessary to achieve success once the others are firmly established. Whatever you're going to do in life, you've got to do it massively! Take massive action on a consistent basis and your results will change. Everything in life is a numbers game. The more often you try, the greater your chances of succeeding at something. Keep going, even when you don't feel like it. Even when faced with death, you will develop a belief system that could save your life.

My college football coach, Cal Stoll, was a person of incredible belief. He lived with another person's heart in his body. He was one of the greatest recruiters in college football history. While coaching at Michigan State under the great Duffy Daugherty, he recruited players such as Bubba Smith, Clinton Jones, and George Webster. He's one of the greatest salesmen I've ever seen.

I called Cal not long ago and teased him about the fact that he coached for four years in the Atlantic Coast Conference and twelve years in the Big Ten and didn't know anything about football. He told me it didn't matter because he believed he would coach big-time college football one day, and belief was all that mattered. His belief allowed him to convince others he could do it, and he did. He then surrounded himself with people who knew what he didn't.

Ironically enough, many of the coaches in the pros today came through his program at the University of Minnesota. Tom Moore, Moe Forte, Tony Dungy, Marc Trestman, and Roger French are all coaches who moved on to great things after being associated with Coach Stoll's program. When Coach Stoll was about to be wheeled into the operating room for his heart transplant, he told the head surgeon, "Look, it's fourth down, we've got the ball on the one-inch line, and there's only one second on the clock. Now, don't screw it up!" He told me he never doubted for one second that he would come out of that operation alive.

Remember, you will not be judged in life by the number of times you fail, but rather by the number of times you succeed. The number of times you succeed is in direct proportion to the number of times you keep trying.

The Principle of Desire

> *I have learned this at least by my experiment: that if one advances confidently in the direction of his dreams, and endeavors to live the life which he has imagined, he will meet with success unexpected in common hours.*
>
> **—Henry David Thoreau**

You must possess an extraordinary amount of desire if you are going to be above average. Desire comes from the inside and can be fueled by your dreams and goals. There is no match for someone who has a burning desire. This comes from having a passion to do something great in life. That's not to say it has to be something that will make you famous or will gain you notoriety; you do it because you love to do it. It will give you a feeling of contribution. When you have enough desire, you won't have to worry much about whether or not you will be successful. You will! A burning fire in your gut will keep you going. You will endure all the temporary setbacks and negative people you will encounter along the way.

A Story of Burning Desire

It was midseason, and Coach Knute Rockne of the University of Notre Dame was hospitalized with phlebitis and a dangerous blood clot in his leg. Notre Dame was slated to play its rival Carnegie Tech. Rockne left his bed to coach the game. He risked his life because he wanted victory more than life. Tom Leed came bursting into the locker room carrying Rockne in his arms as if he were a baby. As he sat Rock on a table, Rockne stared ahead with glassy eyes. The room was silent. The players looked like grade school kids sitting on the benches in front of him. They glanced at the ceiling, bit their lips, and did anything they could to keep the silence from driving them crazy.

It would have been ludicrous if it had not been so serious: the great, strong, fierce, dynamic, indomitable Rockne being carried into the locker room like a baby. There were some wet eyes. You might think this was a very silly business to become so emotional about, but this was Rockne and Notre Dame, it was Stephen and Carnegie Tech. This was the big game!

Behind the lockers, Dr. Maurice Keaney whispered that if Rockne got too excited and that clot released and hit his heart or brain, the chances were even that he'd never leave the locker room alive. These are close to the exact words Rockne said that day: "A lot of water has gone under the bridge, men, since I first came to Notre Dame, but I can't ever remember wanting a game as much as I want this one. Why do you think I'm taking this chance with my life? To see you lose? The other team will be primed, they'll be pumped, they think they've got your number. Are you gonna let it happen again, and again?"

Things got quiet for a moment. The boys' heads were down. Rockne's face was racked with pain. But he had a look of determination. It was the supreme effort of a great fighter. He said, "Go out there and crack 'em, fight 'em, fight to win! You've gotta win, win, win!" As the players roared out of the locker room to take the field, they were yelling and screaming. After the last player left the locker room, Rockne collapsed. The doctor felt his pulse and mopped the sweat from his face. Rockne wanted to win more than he wanted to live. The final score was Notre Dame 7, Carnegie Tech 0. That's what you call desire!

You will know you have a burning desire when you find something that gets you so excited you have trouble sleeping at night, when you can't wait until morning so you can hop out of bed and get on with it. The key is to drive that desire deep by surrounding yourself with all of the positive stimuli you can find—people, books, tapes, and seminars. If you don't have something in your life that compels you at this point, don't despair. Just keep looking. If you look long and hard enough, I promise, you'll find it.

The Principle of Benevolence

> *Consciously and unconsciously, every one of us does render some service or other. If we cultivate the habit of doing this service deliberately, our desire for service will steadily grow stronger, and will make not only for our own happiness but that of the world at large.*
>
> **—Mahatma Gandhi**

I can't tell you how much I've seen this principle manifest itself in my life. I truly believe that the more you give, the more you get out of life. When you learn to give, it spurs reciprocity and will provide all of the help you need in your quest for achievement. I could never find a better example than Osceola McCarty, a ninety-two-year-old washer-woman who lived in Hattiesburg, Mississippi. For years, she squirreled away a portion of the small income she earned washing clothes in her backyard, until she accumulated over $150,000. She then made a personal scholarship endowment to the University of Southern Mississippi of the full amount.

She could have taken that money and spent it on herself. She could have done anything with it, but she decided to give underprivileged students an opportunity to attend college. She was honored by the state of Mississippi and invited to the Congressional Black Caucus dinner as President Clinton's special guest, where she was awarded the Presidential Citizens Medal. There's no doubt she will continue to be blessed in heaven because of her giving heart.

The same will happen for you, too. The more you give, the more you get. The floodgates will open for you in direct proportion to the amount of your giving. Don't ask how much you can get in a situation. Instead, ask how much you can give!

The Principle of Risk Taking

Change and growth take place when a person has risked himself and dares to become involved with experimenting with his own life.

—Herbert Otto

No pain, no gain. No risk, no reward. You've got to be willing to take a chance on you. I've spent a good portion of the money I've earned in life on me. A man at one of my seminars once asked who was bankrolling me. I explained to him that I was bankrolling myself. I told him I will bet on me every time.

It will never be better than it is right now! Take a portion of your time and money and invest it in yourself as often as possible. Too much caution will kill your chances for success.

I realize you can be overzealous and make bad decisions, but ultimately, if things are going to change, you will have to get off your assets and make a decision. Life is so risky that we aren't going to get out of it alive, so why dwell on the worst that can happen? Learn something and move on! Moving in uncharted or unknown waters is always a little hairy, but worse yet is to do nothing but wait for things to happen. You can certainly do your homework before taking a leap of faith, but nothing you can do will ever take every element of risk out of a situation.

Sometimes, life reserves hard knocks for us so we don't forget. Don't run from these lessons; they're coming whether you want them or not. Take them, learn from them, and move forward. If you don't succeed, the worst that can happen is that you will learn something. A wise man was once asked to what he attributed his massive success in life. He said, "I attribute my success to my ability to make good decisions." He was then asked how he learned the art of making good decisions. He said, "I learned the art of making good decisions from my vast array of experience." He was asked how he got all of his experience. He then responded, "From bad decisions!"

The Principle of Honesty

All truth is an achievement. If you would have truth at its value, go win it!

—T. T. Munger

Whatever you do, make sure you are honest in your dealings with other people. You will only be cheating yourself if you aren't. It always catches up with you in the end. Even when you think you've gotten away with something, there's an irrevocable law of nature that always evens the score. Don't try to beat the system. It was here long before you got here, and it will be here long after you're gone.

There are many reasons to be honest. When you do good deeds with good intentions, things will swing back to you the same way. The good fortune will return your way if you do what you know in your heart is right. You never know when you'll need karma to come to your rescue. It will often come when you least expect it.

I once lost my wallet while at a movie theater in Seattle, Washington. I went back later that night to try to retrieve it, but it was too late. I was frantic! I spent the rest of the night cursing mankind. Who would be so cruel as to find someone else's wallet and not return it? I left Seattle and flew back home to Minneapolis, wondering the entire time how much the culprit had attempted to charge on my credit cards.

We sometimes think the worst at first. A few days after I returned home, I received a package from Austin, Texas. A note with it said, "I found your wallet in a theater in Seattle. I hope it comes in handy. I decided it would be best if I mailed it to you. I would have left it at the theater, but I attended the late show and there was no one around to leave it with. Good luck!"

I felt so ashamed. I thought about all of the wallets I had returned to others over the years, and was thankful that the universe had smiled upon me that day. It's not abnormal to think dishonest thoughts; just don't act on them. How many times have you gone into a bank and seen someone counting huge sums of money and wondered what it would be like to reach over the counter and grab a handful?

Honesty is best, I've learned. If and when you must be the bearer of bad news, in the end, people will usually be glad that you told them, particularly if you told them early in the game.

The Principle of Integrity

> *Freedom consists not in refusing to recognize anything above us, but in respecting something which is above; for by respecting it, we raise ourselves to it, and, by our very acknowledgement, prove that we bear within ourselves what is higher, and are worthy to be on a level with it.*
>
> **—Johann Wolfgang von Goethe**

How often do you hire people to do something for you and then find yourself doing a part or all of the work? I once hired a woman to create some promotional material for me and ended up running all over town to make sure things were done properly. The final straw was when I called to ask her about some pictures to be used on my audio albums. She told me she thought I had them. I soon found myself going over to her house to pick up the pictures because she didn't have time to deliver them as she had promised. I wound up talking directly to her vendors to ensure that the project was properly completed.

Needless to say, I no longer deal with her. In fact, I've done myself a huge favor by saving the thousands of dollars I was paying her. The money I spent on her was an investment. By meeting her vendors, I established relationships with people I would never have otherwise met. This will pay dividends for many years to come.

I profited from the experience and used it to gain a greater benefit at a later time. If you're looking to be successful over the long haul, always operate out of integrity. If you say you're going to do something, do it! Even something as trivial as not returning a phone call can cost you major integrity points. People will soon lose faith in you and your goose will be permanently cooked.

The Principle of Resiliency

Our greatest goal must not be in never falling, but arising each time we fall, for, in essence, this is the truest test of all great champions.

—Anonymous

Resiliency is the ability to bounce back after a failure or disappointment. Expect failure to come. Don't worry about getting knocked down. You will! Just make sure you don't stay down. You don't get the chance to fight another day if you pack up your bags and go home.

Many times, people will never know the pain you experienced to get where you are. You can be a star, but nobody will know your potential if you stop going for the goal. If you continue to try, the most important thing is that you will know you are a winner. That's all that counts.

The Greatest Team You'll Never See

In 1977, the University of Minnesota put one of the best teams on the floor in the history of college basketball. The team featured players such as Mychal Thompson (Portland Trail Blazers, Los Angeles Lakers), Kevin McHale (Boston Celtics, Minnesota Timberwolves), Ray Williams (New York Knicks, Boston Celtics), Osborne Lockhart (Harlem Globetrotters), and Phil "Flip" Saunders (Minnesota Timberwolves). This team went 24–3 that year and was one of the best in the country.

The team was so good that Marquette University, which later won the NCAA tournament that year, had lost to the University of Minnesota by more than thirty points on their home court in Milwaukee. During the NCAA tournament, Al McGuire, the famed coach of the Marquette Warriors, said that the best team in the country was not in the tournament. Minnesota was not allowed to go to the tournament because they were on probation for alleged recruiting violations. What was so impressive was to see these guys go out every night and lay it all on the line when there was supposedly nothing to play for, since they were eliminated from tournament play. They made each team they played feel the wrath of their frustration.

Although the Gophers were barred from the "Big Show," there was no doubt they left an indelible mark on the sport. They demonstrated an incredible amount of resiliency. They fought all year as though they would play in the tournament—a testament to their character. You can get the same results from your own life. Whatever level you strive to achieve, there will be challenges at that level to greet you. Just remember: the greater the challenge, the more glorious the victory!

The Principle of Forgiveness

I like the dreams of the future better than the history of the past.

—Thomas Jefferson

This is a powerful life principle that will free your spirit. Spite and resentfulness will destroy you. Trust me on this one—I know! I spent most of my life hating my mother. I hated her for the kind of life she led and for the kind of life I had to experience as a result. I suppose she felt the same way. We went for thirty years without seeing each other more than a dozen times. I knew I loved her, but bitterness wouldn't allow me to make contact.

It makes me sad now to think that thirty years went by without my mother in my life. As I got more involved in my speaking and training business, I kept having a feeling of hollowness and incongruity. Here I was, talking to other people throughout the country about their personal development, and yet I had not gotten my own house in order. I knew that was hypocritical. That feeling kept gnawing at me. I knew I had to do something about it.

One Friday night, I happened to be in Orange County, California, conducting a seminar for Baxter/Kraft Food Service. The next morning, after much deliberation, I called my mother, who'd moved to Los Angeles from St. Louis when I was in high school. I was sweating bullets.

We talked on the phone for two hours, catching up. Finally, she told me she had to go because her ride to church had arrived. I thought, "Church? We hardly ever went to church when I lived at home." There was something different about her. I hadn't seen her since 1982 because it hurt so badly to see her on drugs. Sometimes my mother would be so high on speed, marijuana, sherm, or prescription drugs that it would take her a while to recognize me. She would then spring to her feet and call my name, "Desi, Desi, Desi! This is my son, you all!" I would cry for days afterward.

This time, I realized things had changed. I had changed. I was ready to make peace with the past and move on to a brighter future for the both of us. After telling me she had to go, she asked me to give her the phone number where I was. I told her to let me know what time she would be home. I wanted to surprise her with a visit. I had to hold myself together enough to make the two-hour drive to South-Central Los Angeles. I noticed people looking at me as I drove toward the City of Angels, which I'd often considered the City of Hell because of what had happened to my family there: My brother was in the pen, and my mother and sister had fallen prey to the fast life. People were looking at me because I was sobbing uncontrollably. I let rip some feelings for years gone by; it was time to let it all out. This was going to be a day of healing old wounds.

I had attempted to go by her house many times in the past, but I really hadn't wanted to find it, for fear of what I might discover when I got there. This day was different. My mother and I had become different people. I could feel it over the phone. I knew the time was right to practice some of the things I was teaching other people: persistence, forgiveness, and benevolence. I was committed to finding her house this time. Several times I got lost and asked for directions. Eventually, I found myself edging closer to areas I recognized. My heart began to pound. I made a couple of turns and read a sign: Bangor Street. I knew her house was the last one on the right.

As I pulled up to her house, I could feel sweat run down my arms. I hopped out of the car, ran to the front door, and rang the doorbell. It was as if my mother had X-ray vision. I could hear her screaming, "Oh my God! It's my baby!" When she opened the door, we embraced. I could say only four words, and I said them over and over again: "I love you, Mama." My mother kept repeating, "I love you, son."

We went inside and talked for five hours. We spread pictures over the floor and caught up on thirty years. I surprised her when I told her she had a granddaughter and grandson. She cried when I showed her their pictures. Then she said something enormously important. "Son, I'm sorry for all of the things that happened," she said. "I couldn't give you love because I never had anybody love me. I couldn't give you what I didn't have. I never knew my father, and my stepfather raped, beat, and took advantage of me constantly when I was a young girl. I've spent the last thirty years in a mad search to find myself, and, through Jesus Christ, I've been able to do it. I love you, Desi. I've always loved you! I'll always be your mama. No matter what happens, nothing will ever change that." I called my father while I was there and put the two of them on the phone. They hadn't talked to each other in more than thirty years. Seeing her on that phone was a beautiful sight.

I felt guilty for judging her all of those years. I didn't know the hell she had been through in her life. I was too young to understand when I ran away. I didn't have the right to condemn her for the rest of her life because she didn't live up to my expectations. I had never walked a mile in her shoes.

Think about how often you judge someone harshly without knowing what that person has to deal with. I always think about the biblical phrase "Let he who is without sin cast the first stone."

When I got into the car for the drive back to Orange County, I cried harder than I've ever cried in my life. But this time, I was crying out of joy. A great weight had been lifted from my shoulders. We were finally free to love each other unconditionally. I felt like a complete man for the first time in my life. My mother came to Minneapolis to visit her grandchildren that fall, and my wife finally became acquainted with a part of my life that had always been a mystery.

What's in Your Black Box?

By Federal Aviation Administration regulations, all aircraft must have a flight recorder on board known as the black box. After every plane crash, authorities scramble to find this box because it contains valuable information and history: the problems and root causes that explain why the plane's systems or pilots failed. From there, precautions can be implemented to prevent future crashes. If the black box is not retrieved, it is impossible to ascertain the problems from an inside perspective, and authorities must investigate further and speculate as to the causes associated with the crash.

On this flight called life, I believe we each have a little black box that contains our past. In it, there are tapes that play constantly inside our heads. Some of them record terrible experiences from our past that if not retrieved and dealt with will cause us great pain throughout our lives. Every time we seek to move ahead, recordings from certain incidents pop on and play clear and vivid pictures of these negative situations. We experience the full emotional range, as if it's happening right now.

For me, there was a specific tape I had buried long ago because the pain was always too great. The tape was that of sexual abuse. The pictures were clear and resonant. When I was four years old, a lady named Miss Hayes was my baby-sitter. She was a kind and gentle woman who trusted her son Frank to watch me one day while she went to the store. He took me into the basement of their home and sexually abused me. I can remember it just like it was yesterday. I never told anyone. I kept it stashed in my little black box. I was always too ashamed to mention it. It made me feel dirty and unworthy.

I vowed that when I became a man, if I ever saw him, I would kill him. I didn't have the courage to include this story in the first edition of this book because I was not yet healed. I thought something was wrong with me. I must have been a bad little boy to deserve something so injurious.

Many times, as I would attempt to raise myself up emotionally from my troubled past, the thought of this terrible event would raise its ugly head. The more often it did, the deeper I would push it into my black box. I could never enjoy my successes fully and always regarded my failures as some kind of just punishment.

One day I met my past head-on. It had been a long, humid summer, as summers in St. Louis go. I had been running errands with my father the entire morning as we prepared his bar and restaurant for another day. When I walked into the bar from the kitchen, the music blasted, and the cigarette smoke was so thick you could cut it with a knife.

At the end of the bar, a familiar silhouette sat slumped over the bar. Although I could not see him clearly through the people and confusion, I knew who it was. Boom! I flashed back to that awful day in that basement thirty-four years before. I didn't know what to do. If I told my father, he would kill him, no question. I thought about killing him myself.

The years since the incident had blessed me with size and mass that made me an imposing figure compared to this scrawny-looking man, a man who had appeared much larger than life when he sexually abused me. I could easily have killed him with my bare hands.

I went to meet my assailant face-to-face. I wanted to hold him accountable. I was filled with anger and vengeance. I prayed, "Father God, please walk with me, handle this for me, it's too big for me to tackle alone."

I didn't know what would happen once I reached the end of that bar. I could feel my hands tighten around his throat, him gasping for air. Payback for all my years of suffering! But something strange happened. The closer I got to him, the more a calming presence took control. It was the voice of God Almighty himself telling me to, through him, handle this situation in a different way.

When I got face-to-face with Frank, it was obvious that life had dealt him the hand he deserved. He was a beaten man who looked far older than his years. He could barely meet my eyes. He was also shaking hands with his past as he sat there. Beating him up wouldn't change him or what had happened, and would only lessen me as a man. He was already beaten by life.

I surprised myself and calmly sat down. My father, not knowing what had happened, came over and asked me if I remembered Frank. My dad and mother had rented from Miss Hayes when I was a baby. He had known Frank all that time. When he left us, I told Frank I remembered him, but for all the wrong reasons. As painful as it was, I told him of the terrible effect his act had had on my life growing up. He sat there in shock, speechless, as he met, point-blank, with personal responsibility and accountability. God had spoken to me that day. He'd said, "Let me handle this my way. I've already taken care of it." I was perfectly calm-looking outside, but inside I was shaking, and my heart pounded—bad intentions held in check by my Creator. God saved both of our lives that day.

I told Frank I wanted to kill him but that instead I would hold him accountable for his actions, that I would pray for him, and that I'd forgiven him. This had a far greater impact on him than any beating. It was now between him and a power more capable than I of dealing with it.

I've faced many of those old recordings in my little black box of life; not totally erasing them, but reducing their power and control over my life. It has freed me. It will do the same for you. What's on the tape in your little black box?

I challenge you to deal with these tapes once and for all. Confront the situations and the people involved, with the loving hand of God guiding you. Ask for his intervention, and trust that, through him, you will handle it properly. As you truly forgive, the memory of these situations will have less impact. You may never forget, but you will find that you've given yourself special gifts: love, reverence, humility, active faith, and, ultimately, the freedom to soar to new heights because the tapes on the flight recorder of your life will no longer be your slave master but rather your servant. You will sit on the tarmac of a brighter and better future, ready to take off toward deeper self-understanding and personal development.

Be a Healer

I encourage you to become a catalyst for healing in your own life. If there's someone out there you are harboring negative feelings about, pick up the phone, call them, and heal the problem. There is risk involved. A bigger risk is living with the regret and pain that will come if you don't. What prompted me to repair my past with my mother was the fact that many of my friends had lost their parents after years of bad relationships. The one thing they all said, with tears in their eyes, was that they'd never had a chance to tell their parents they loved them. They'd had the opportunity; they just hadn't taken it, and now they were living with regret. They would never have the chance to rectify the situation, because they'd waited too long.

I don't want you to blow it. Whether you realize it or not, this kind of burden affects every area of your life. If you're not as successful as you'd like to be, healing old wounds like this will help free your spirit and clear your head so you can focus on your goals. If you feel you're already successful, it will help you become more successful as you create more balance in your life.

I want you to pick up the phone and call the people in question. Tell them you want to let them know you are sorry for whatever it was that happened between you, even if it wasn't your fault. Tell them you love them, how important they are to you, and how much you miss them. Tell them you want to forget about the past and have the best relationship you can have with them from this day forward.

Whether these people respond positively or negatively is not critical. What's most important is what it will do for you. You will have opened the door for the other person to walk through. Don't despair, for they may not have reached the level of emotional maturity you have at this point. When they're ready, they will come around. You will find, more often than not, that the person in question will be feeling the same way you do. They just didn't have the confidence or courage to put their finger on the buttons and call.

If things are going to change, someone has to take charge. I promise that taking an active role in forgiving others will change your life forever. I can tell you that it worked for me. Why not give it a try?

CHAPTER 11
BRINGING IT HOME

Onward

*Every ending is a new
beginning! Life is an endless
unfoldment.*

*New opportunities give you
chances to win . . . again!
Some way you'll find atonement.*

*Meet your new challenges and
goals with optimism and
determination.*

*Stand ready to liven up yourself
if it's rough going and you
need motivation.*

**Set sail!
Do well!
It's time to excel!**

—Saunni Dais

> *Such gardens are not made*
> *By singing:—"Oh, how beautiful!" and sitting in the shade.*
>
> **—Rudyard Kipling**

There's no question about it. You play the primary role in how things turn out in your life. It is my hope and dream that you have found some inspiration, motivation, and answers in what I'm saying. My goal has been to give you an unparalleled amount of value for each. If you feel this has happened, both of us have richly benefited.

The Lord said, "If you will plant the seed, I will provide the blessing of the sun, the seed, the soil, and the rain." This means you must now go out and do something about what you've learned, what you know, and how you feel.

There's a story about a farmer who took an awful-looking piece of land. There was glass, trash, rocks, and debris everywhere. This place was truly a mess. He took it and—*whoosh!*—transformed it into a beautiful farm and garden. There were rows and rows of corn, wheat, and soybeans. There were rows and rows of flowers, of all shapes and sizes. He had horses that could run like the wind. The farmhouse was beautiful, with perfectly manicured grounds. This place was really something special.

One day, a jealous neighbor stopped by to compliment the farmer on how beautiful this place looked, but he didn't want to give the farmer too much credit for this incredible transformation. He said, "My, my, what a beautiful farm and garden the Lord has blessed you with!" The farmer became a little perturbed by the cynical manner in which the neighbor delivered his praise. The farmer said, "You know something? You're right: If it wasn't for the Lord and the blessing of the soil, the seed, the sun, and the rain, there would certainly be no farm and no garden either. But let me tell you something, Jack: You should have seen this place when the Lord had it all by himself!"

You must get off your assets and do something. Everything you need is already within your reach. You've got everything it takes to be a winner inside you right now. Most of all, you've got the winning spirit. What I want you to do from this day forward is unleash that spirit and let it explode.

Apollinaire said:

"Come to the edge!"
They said, "It's too high!"
He said, "Come to the edge!"
They said, "We might fall!"
He said, "Come to the edge!"
And they came.
And he pushed them.
And they flew!

—Christopher Hogue

UNLEASH THE POWER IN YOU!

ACTION GUIDE FOR PERSONAL ACHIEVEMENT

Mission

To aid you in personal growth and development by offering solutions and ideas to assist you as you strive to achieve results in all areas of your life.

This action guide will provide you with the self-empowerment and personal-development skills necessary to discover and maximize your potential while achieving happiness, success, and more control over the conditions in your life.

In this action guide, you will learn how to:

- Program your mind for success.
- Change your life for the better.
- Use the power of personal development.
- Set goals that will change your life.
- Create a winning attitude.
- Discover core values that will change your life.

SECTION ONE:
YOUR CURRENT REALITY

Ask Yourself:

Are you happy with your current situation in life? With your career or business?

_____

_____

_____

What's good about your life? You business or career?

_____

_____

_____

Do you want to do more with your life or business than you are?

_____

_____

_____

What would you like to change?

_____

_____

_____

What would it take to make you feel successful in life?

_____

_____

_____

In business? In your career?

_____

_____

_____

What are your abilities? Your potential? Why? Please explain.

_____

_____

_____

Do you have firm beliefs and stick to them? Please explain.

_____

_____

_____

Do you take good care of your health?

_____

_____

_____

When you fail or make a mistake, do you learn from it?

_____

_____

_____

Do you communicate and express yourself well? Please explain.

_____

_____

_____

The Power of Adjustment

When winners make mistakes, they don't see them as failures but as ways to learn to make better decisions for future success.

Most people give up at the first sign of opposition. Winners never take rejection personally; they keep going until they succeed.

When you made a mistake or were rejected in the past:

What did you learn from it?

_____

_____

_____

How would you handle it the next time?

_____

_____

_____

What adjustments would you make?

_____

_____

_____

_____

How would you use what you've learned in the future?

_____

_____

_____

_____

The Power of Personal Identity

Your personal identity is the foundation of your life. It determines your self-image. Self-image is what you believe to be true about yourself. It determines your level of self-confidence and comfort with the outside world.

Here, don't describe yourself by explaining who you are as a person. Instead answer this question: If we were attending your funeral, what would you want said about you? What effect did you have on the world? What was your gift to the world?

_____

_____

_____

_____

_____

The Power of Purpose

Purpose is often created by something that compels us to take action. A personal challenge will give you a reason to get up early and stay up late. It's like rocket fuel for life.

Exercise:

What is your purpose? What do you want to do with your life? Business? Career? What would you have as a purpose if you knew you couldn't fail?

_____

_____

_____

_____

_____

_____

Reasons for Succeeding

You must learn to act on life or it will act on you.

We all have something we feel so strongly about that we would be willing to lay our lives on the line for it. When you find a purpose in life you feel strongly about, you will find a way to accomplish it!

The key to discovering your purpose is to ask the question "Why?" This causes all kinds of mental machinery to start working for you. It's like pressing the "on" button for a huge conveyor belt that will bring you vital answers to the questions you need to examine to make life-changing decisions.

Exercise:

In the spaces below, compose a list of reasons for succeeding that are so compelling they cause you to get excited about your future. First list the reason, then why you want to achieve it.

1. _____

_____

_____

2. _____

_____

_____

3. _____

_____

_____

4. _____

_____

_____

5. _____

_____

_____

The key is to be perfectly honest with yourself.

The Power of Thought

Winners in personal life, business, and career use lessons from the past to create an even better future for themselves. You can, too! You must learn from the past and use it as a launching pad to the future.

Exercise:

Think of a time you talked yourself out of doing something because you thought you couldn't do it. Write it down. How did it make you feel?

_____

_____

_____

_____

_____

_____

Think back to a time when you didn't do something you now regret. How often do you think about it? How does it make you feel?

_____

_____

_____

_____

_____

_____

List something major in your life that you are absolutely committed to changing right now. Write down how you plan to do it.

It's not what happens to you that will determine how your life turns out; it's what you do about it that makes the difference! **Now take a few minutes to fill in your thoughts below.**

Insight: What you've learned about your purpose in personal life, family, business, career:

Action: What you're going to do:

SECTION TWO:
THE POWER OF INFLUENCE

Exercise:

Make a list of people you have known or read about who represent a positive example of how to live successfully.

_____

_____

_____

_____

_____

Make a list of people you have known or read about who represent what not to do in life.

_____

_____

_____

_____

_____

What lessons did you learn from both examples listed above? How can you use both to change your life for the better?

_____

_____

_____

_____

_____

Exercise:

What are some of the things you are going to do about the people who negatively influence you?

_____

_____

_____

_____

_____

_____

The Power of Vision

We must make a conscious effort to control our thoughts, continue to develop a larger vision of ourselves, and see ourselves doing the things that will help us to realize our dreams.

Pretend that you are watching a computer screen and looking at your behavior. List some of the ways you have been an obstacle in accomplishing your goals and ways you can be the solution.

_____

_____

_____

_____

_____

Close your eyes for three minutes and dream about what you would like to become. See yourself accomplishing the task. See yourself massively successful. What do you see? How does it feel? Write down your answers.

_____

_____

_____

_____

_____

We are constantly influenced by the things we hear and see. List some of the things you have seen or heard in the last week that have affected you. List whether the effects were positive or negative. List how you can better accentuate the positives and minimize the negatives in your life.

_____

_____

_____

_____

_____

_____

Insight: What you've learned:

_____

_____

_____

Action: What you're going to do:

_____

_____

_____

For you to get off the treadmill of desperation and reach your goals, you must be willing to invest time in being uncomfortable. The comfort zone is a dangerous place to be, for you will never realize your true potential until you test the limits of your being.

SECTION THREE:
HOW TO PROGRAM YOUR MIND

Exercise:

Many people don't do well because they constantly focus on the negative things in life rather than the positive. Below, list something negative, and then next to it list at least three positive things. They can be anything. There are no rules.

Negative   **Positive**

1.   1.

                                  2.

                                  3.

2.   1.

                                  2.

                                  3.

3.   1.

                                  2.

                                  3.

4.   1.

                                  2.

                                  3.

Moral: If you had trouble listing more positive things than negative, you simply need to change your focus so that you look for the good things in life even when something bad happens. Ask yourself a question: What's good about this? Remember, you get what you focus on in life.

The Three Components of Human Interaction

Communication skills are important for success in your personal and family life, business, and your career. You must be able to express yourself well. The quality of your communication will determine the quality of your life. In the spaces below, estimate what percentage these qualities of communication represent. (Answers are listed on page 208.)

Words (what you say):

Your estimate _____%   Actual _____%

Tone and pace (how you say what you say):

Your estimate _____%   Actual _____%

Physiology (how you use your body when you talk, including gestures, facial expression, volume, speed, tempo, eye contact, body spacing):

Your estimate _____%   Actual _____%

List three ways in which you will increase your communication skills over the next year.

_____

_____

_____

_____

_____

Self-Talk

What you say to yourself has a definite impact on how you think and what you do. It affects your performance as well as the results you get from life.

How do you feel about yourself when you've accomplished something you've set out to do? What do you say to yourself?

_____

_____

_____

_____

_____

_____

How do you feel about yourself when you've failed at something you've tried? What do you say to yourself?

_____

_____

_____

_____

_____

_____

Exercise:

What did you learn about yourself?

From now on I will . . .

_____

_____

My life is better because . . .

_____

_____

When I succeed, I feel . . .

_____

_____

I love to win because . . .

_____

_____

I will increase my skill level because . . .

_____

_____

I will be successful because . . .

_____

_____

GET OFF YOUR ASSETS!

I am a smart, capable person who will . . .

_____

_____

From this point on I will never again . . .

_____

_____

I'm looking forward to . . .

_____

_____

I am the one who determines my . . .

_____

_____

One day I'm going to be . . .

_____

_____

I will positively impact the world by . . .

_____

_____

I will help others by . . .

_____

_____

I will continue to develop my skills by . . .

_____

_____

I will become a better person by . . .

_____

_____

I will develop better health habits by . . .

_____

_____

I will become a better leader by . . .

_____

_____

I will acquire better reading skills because . . .

_____

_____

I will dream bigger dreams because . . .

_____

_____

Exercise:

Insight: What you've learned:

_____

_____

_____

_____

_____

_____

Action: What you're going to do:

_____

_____

_____

_____

_____

_____

SECTION FOUR:
HOW TO HELP YOURSELF

Personal-Development Power

Personal development is the starting point for all achievement. You can learn new skills and develop a positive mind-set that will eliminate the behavior that has held you back in the past. You have the ability to decide exactly how your life will turn out.

When you finally decide to take responsibility for your growth and development, your life will change and you will take quantum leaps compared to what you've done in the past. You must actively seek out knowledge in its various forms and never stop learning.

Exercise:

Fill in the missing blanks to the following questions regarding the subject of personal development. (Answers are listed on page 208.)

We get paid for the _____ we create in the marketplace.

Things get better when _____ get better.

In order for things to change, _____ going to have to change.

The major key to my better future is _____.

I can have more than I have because I can _____ more than I am.

If it's to be, it's up to _____ .

I don't get paid for _____, I get paid for _____ .

There are two kinds of education, _____ and _____ .

How much money I earn is a direct reflection of my _____ _____ .

If I continue to do what I've always done, I'll continue to have what I've _____ .

The Power of Learning

There's formal education and self-education. Formal education comes from our school system. Self-education is when you actively pursue knowledge on your own. This is a real act of maturity that will mark the beginning of your better future.

It doesn't matter how successful you have been in the past; you must seek to continue your education so that you remain a valuable commodity in the marketplace. You must continually expand your knowledge base in order to remain on the cutting edge of coming changes.

Learn how to communicate.

- Expand your vocabulary.
- Learn how to say it well.
- Learn how to speak in groups.

Learn to observe.

- Become a student of lifelong learning.
- Become a reader (spend at least one hour a day).
- Learn from the past.
- Make life a study.

Associate with successful people.

- Learn from successful people.
- Look at how they did it.
- Adopt some of their positive traits.

Become a student.

- Success leaves clues.
- Get around successful people and listen.
- Ask questions; listen more than you talk.

Get excited about your life.

- Be curious like a child.
- Look forward to learning new things.
- Wake up each day with an attitude of gratitude.

Exercise:

What is it you really want to learn? What will you do to ensure that you learn it? How much time do you spend each day reading?

_____

_____

_____

_____

_____

List people you admire and are going to ask to be your mentors so you can learn from them. Whom do you admire who has written books or made audio- or videotapes you could use to become a student of their philosophy?

_____

_____

_____

_____

_____

Explain why you think it's important to listen to other people, particularly those with more knowledge in a given area than yourself.

_____

_____

_____

_____

_____

What is it about your life you feel grateful for? How will you take this feeling and use it to your advantage?

_____

_____

_____

_____

_____

List three things you need to do over the course of the next few years to improve yourself, and what steps you're going to take to make them happen.

_____

_____

_____

_____

_____

Time Management

If you really want to do well in life, you must make sure you maintain very close control over your time. You must not allow yourself to spend major time on minor things.

If you want to make quantum leaps in your own individual progress, you must make the decision to do the most productive thing possible at every given moment. You will find that most successful people don't spend their time watching television eight hours a day. Their time is too valuable! You must learn that your time is your most valuable commodity. When you do, you will be taking a very important step toward increasing the quality of your life.

Exercise:

Below, list the ways in which you use your time performing various activities outside of work or school.

Example:

Activity	Number of Hours Spent per Week
Watching television	20
Reading	16
Playing sports	20
Visiting with friends	10
Week's total	66

Activity	Number of Hours Spent per Week
Week's total	

Review the activities you have listed above. Beside each activity, write the number of hours that it contributes to your personal development. Add up the hours you have entered and write the total in the space below.

Total hours devoted to personal development: _____ hours

You need to make sure your life is balanced with activities that address your needs. It's important to spend time relaxing and enjoying yourself.

Total unproductive hours: _____ hours

If you find you are not spending any time on personal development, imagine what would happen if you decided to start spending five, ten, or fifteen hours a week on increasing your skills. What if you set aside one hour a day for reading? What would happen if you really spent quality time on your work assignments rather than rushing to get finished so you could indulge yourself in playtime? The difference in the rewards you will get will be tremendous!

Ask not what it costs, but what it's worth. We must be willing to give up something in order to get something. It's not a question of having time, because there's plenty. How will you use yours from this day forward?

Exercise:

What activities could you give up that would provide you with more time to spend working on your personal-development program? List the activities you could possibly sacrifice, how many hours you would free up by doing so, and how you could better use the time.

_____

_____

_____

_____

_____

_____

_____

Total hours available:

_____

How many hours could you now spend on a personal-development program? _____ hours

In what ways do you feel this would build a better life?

Insight: What you've learned:

_____

_____

_____

_____

_____

Action: What you're going to do:

_____

_____

_____

_____

_____

Your life can be whatever you choose to make of it, for just over the horizon is the better life that awaits you. It's all predicated upon you becoming more today than you were yesterday, and more tomorrow than you are today.

—Desi Williamson

Section Five:
Goal Power

Without goals, you will drift through life. When you set goals, you take charge of your life and decide what you want, when you want it, and how you plan to accomplish it. Goals will make you a better person, not so much for what you get at the end, but for what you become to achieve them.

With goals, you design your life the way you want it. They can revolutionize the possibilities for your future. To achieve success, you must plan it; rarely do things of significance happen by chance. By breaking larger goals into smaller ones, you gain confidence and reward yourself along the way. Your goals must involve honesty and integrity and must benefit others as well as yourself.

There are certain rules of the goal-setting process that must be followed:

The Rule of Six in Goal Setting

- Goals must be **WRITTEN.** This shows that you are serious about your future. Most people spend more time planning a vacation than they do their lives. What are your goals for you personally? As a family member? In business? In your career?

- Goals must be **SPECIFIC.** It's not enough to merely say, "I want to get my degree." A better way to put it would be, "I will earn a degree from the University of [Your Choice] by attending class regularly and applying myself to the best of my abilities. I will graduate in the spring of 2020." You can even be more specific by listing the month, day, and year in which you will reach an objective.

- Goals must be **MOTIVATIONAL.** Your goals must be based on something you feel excited about. What do you enjoy doing? What do you dream of doing or becoming? What do you enjoy doing so much you would do it for free (outside of sports)?

- Goals must be **ATTAINABLE.** Give yourself a chance to win! Set larger goals and break them into smaller parts that are more easily achieved. For example, if your goal was to become a millionaire, you would set the goal by 1) getting your high school education; 2) deciding what college or trade school to attend in order to develop your skills; 3) finding work in your chosen field or perhaps starting your own business; 4) picking a set amount of money to set aside each month for investment until you've reached your goal.

- Goals must be **RELEVANT.** They must be something you feel strongly about. They must be important enough to grab your full attention.

- Goals must be **TRACEABLE.** If you don't know how you're doing, you'll never know when you get there! How are you doing over the short term? Long term?

The Four Categories of Goals

- **Values of goals.** Values guide every decision you make. They are the principles that determine how you live your life. What's most important to you in life? Ask the same question about your education, job, family, friends, health, or any other subject.

- **Short-range goals.** These represent the things you would like to accomplish in the next one, three, or five years in order to reach your destination. Short-range goals can also be broken down into weeks or months to help you to realize your dreams. Understand what's most important in the short term so that you do the most productive things at the right time.

- **Long-range goals.** These represent the things you would like to accomplish in the next ten, fifteen, or twenty years. What do you see yourself doing at more mature stages of your life? Where would you like to be living? What kind of things would you like to have?

- **Daily task goals.** These are the things you do on a daily basis that ultimately determine your destiny. It is suggested that you plan each day of your life out as carefully as possible with a "to do" list. There's a big difference between urgent things and the most important things. Urgent things often distract us from the things that will really help us move forward.

Exercise:

The following values exercise will help you determine some of the things that are most important to you in life. List the top twenty things most important to you. Place an "M" next to the ones that require money, place a "P" next to the ones that require the participation of others, and place a date next to each entry to determine when you want it. Finally, prioritize the list by determining your "top ten" values.

It's important to note there are no rights or wrongs. These are your values and yours alone.

1._____   11. _____

2._____   12. _____

3._____   13. _____

4._____   14. _____

5._____   15. _____

6._____   16. _____

7._____   17. _____

8._____   18. _____

9._____   19. _____

10._____   20. _____

What did you learn about yourself from this exercise?

_____

_____

_____

_____

_____

_____

Refer to these values when setting your long-range and short-range goals. They will help give more meaning to your goals and help keep you focused on what's most important.

Dream Big Dreams!

Exercise:

Take two minutes to relax, close your eyes, and dream about the things you would like to have happen in your life. What would you like to become? What would you like to have? Where would you like to travel? Think about your top ten values as you dream. How do they influence what you dream about for your future?

_____

_____

_____

_____

_____

_____

Take five minutes to list as many goals as you can. Don't try to spend too much time thinking about them; just write as many of them down as you can get within the next five minutes. No matter what, keep your pen moving.

_____

_____

_____

_____

_____

Rule: What would you set as a goal if you knew you couldn't fail? If you can dream it, you can do it! Ready . . . ?

_____

_____

_____

_____

_____

_____

_____

_____

_____

Short-Range Goal Commitments

Exercise:

List each of your short-range goals for one, three, and five years. Make sure you keep them in proper sequence. Write a short statement as to what date in the coming year(s) you will accomplish these objectives. For example:

Goal: Read twenty-four books in the coming year.

Statement: I will read at least twenty-four books in the coming year, and this will be accomplished by: month, day, year.

You could go further and break this goal down by month and list each book you plan to read and by what date.

_____

_____

_____

_____

_____

_____

_____

Long-Range Goals

Exercise:

Go back to your original list of dream goals and place a 10, 15, or 20 next to the goals you feel you can accomplish in that many years.

_____

_____

_____

_____

_____

_____

_____

_____

Long-Range Goal Commitments

Exercise:

Long-range goals don't need to be as specific as short-range ones because, as time passes, they will eventually become short-range goals. Take each of your long-range goals and write a commitment statement as to when you will achieve your ten-, fifteen-, or twenty-year goals. It is not necessary to write the month or day, but only the year in which you will have achieved a particular goal.

Goal: To become a nationally known author.

Statement: I will be known throughout the country as an author of books for self-development and self-empowerment by 2010.

Daily-Task Goals

When you plan your activities, you will find that you maintain more control over your time and operate more efficiently if you know your goals in advance. By committing your task to paper, you are reinforcing in your own mind the importance of your actions.

Break your tasks into:

Quarters

Weeks

Days

Note: Always keep your goals somewhere that allows you to look at them as often as possible. A binder or day planner is best. The more you review them, the better chance you have of keeping them in the "top of your mind" and actually accomplishing them. Remember: The person who fails is planning to fail.

Insight: What you've learned:

_____

_____

_____

_____

_____

_____

Action: What you're going to do:

_____

_____

_____

_____

_____

_____

SECTION SIX:
YOUR ATTITUDE

Adjusting Your Attitude

The amount of happiness, success, and personal development you experience in life is a direct reflection of your attitude. The brighter your outlook, the greater your chances of achieving your goal.

You can choose the way you think, which will ultimately determine how you feel. Your feelings will transform into actions, and your actions will determine your destiny.

You must take inventory of everything that affects your life, including your goals, the people who influence you, what you watch, what you read, what you listen to, and how you think about your life.

Believe in Yourself, For I Believe in You!

Beliefs are powerful medicine for motivation. They are the compass and road map that will direct you to your outcome. Our beliefs are a matter of choice. What you believe comes from a variety of sources, such as your environment, experiences, knowledge, wisdom, and past results. When you believe in yourself and the possibilities in your life, you create in your mind the outcome you desire in the future, as if it were happening now. It's important to understand that the power of self-belief is enormous. There is greatness in you! Why not give yourself every opportunity to succeed? The biggest mountains you will ever have to climb are in your own mind.

Exercise:

In the space below, list at least five major events in your life that have affected you the most.

_____

_____

_____

_____

_____

Exercise:

Knowledge: Below, list five positive things you've learned from books you've read or people who have taught you something.

_____

_____

_____

_____

Exercise:

Past Experience: List five things you have come to believe that derived from your personal experiences.

_____

_____

_____

_____

Exercise:

Resiliency: One of the most powerful skills is the ability to bounce back from disappointments. This is the difference between winning and losing. Describe a time you were disappointed in an outcome in your life and how you bounced back from it.

_____

_____

_____

_____

_____

Exercise:

The **Philosophy of "Next"** is important in helping you move from a position of being stuck, to one of massive action. Describe something that's got you stuck. What are you going to do to move yourself forward?

_____

_____

_____

_____

_____

Exercise:

Persistence: Describe a time when you quit at something you wanted to do. Also note at least two new ways to approach the accomplishment of this goal.

_____

_____

_____

_____

_____

Exercise:

Disgust: Describe something you are really disgusted about in your life and what you will do to make a difference.

_____

_____

_____

_____

_____

Exercise:

Resolve: Describe something you are absolutely committed to doing to ensure that you become a better person tomorrow. Promise yourself that you will do whatever it takes to make it happen.

_____

_____

_____

_____

_____

Exercise:

Forgiveness: Write down the name of someone you are not on good terms with or describe something that has happened that causes you to harbor bad feelings. Also list what steps you are going to take to change this situation and make it right so you can move forward.

_____

_____

_____

_____

_____

Exercise:

Passion: List something you are passionate about and what you will do about it in the future.

_____

_____

_____

_____

_____

Exercise:

Insight: What you've learned:

_____

_____

_____

_____

_____

Action: What you're going to do:

_____

_____

_____

_____

_____

Answers

Answers to exercise on page 179:

Words: The actual words you speak make up only 7 percent of the impact of what you say.

Tone and pace: The tone and pace of your voice contribute 38 percent to the impact of what you say.

Physiology: The positioning of your body while you speak carries 55 percent of the impact of what you say.

Answers to exercise on pages 185–186:

value

I

I'm

me

become

me

time, value

formal, self

skill level

got

Dear Reader,

I've dedicated my life to helping people unleash the power within themselves. You can do remarkable things in life because you are a remarkable person. The key is to get it started; then make it a point to watch over the course of your life as a mother hen does her chicks. When you take charge of your life and plan it according to your purpose, values, goals, dreams, and take massive action, you will seldom be surprised by the outcome. Go for it!

I wish you the "best of success." Have a great life!

Best regards,

Desi Williamson

Desi Williamson

Faith

Doubt sees the obstacle,
Faith sees the way.
Doubt sees the darkest night,
Faith sees the day.
Doubt fails to take a step,
Faith just soars on high.
Doubt asks, "Who believes?"
Faith answers, "I!"

—Anonymous

Time is the most valuable commodity on earth. Unlike other resources, you can't save it, stop it, or change it. The only thing you can do with time is use it!

—Desi Williamson